TARGET GERMANY

CAVENDISH HOUSE

Published by
Marshall Cavendish Limited
58 Old Compton Street
London WV1 5PA

© Marshall Cavendish Limited 1974-83

ISBN 0 86307 155 4
Printed in Yugoslavia

TARGET GERMANY

Contents

FLYING FORTRESS

It climbed above German flak and fighters. From 30,000ft the Fort's bombs pin-pointed targets in Germany's war industry

At 30,000ft B17s of 390th Bomber Group, 13th Wing, head towards their target. Above them, alert Mustang P51B escorts weave vapor-trail patterns in the deep blue sky. Vapor trails were caused through the condensation of hot exhaust gases.

'The more Fortresses we have, the shorter the war is going to be.' This was the confident prediction of Curtis E. LeMay, commander of the 305th Bombardment Group, based in England in 1943. He was referring to the American B17 Flying Fortress heavy bomber. Cruising high in the daylight skies of the Reich, the Flying Fortress brought the bombing power of the Allies home to the German people—something that the previous night raids of the British RAF had not achieved. From the modest beginnings in late 1942, when a few score bombers raided Germany, the bomber assault on the Reich had been transformed by February 1944, when a thousand bombers filled the skies over Berlin, a full 10 hours flying time from the English bases. Hitler had boasted of his European Fortress, *Festung Europa*. But the B17s proved the truth of Roosevelt's retort: 'Hitler forgot to put a roof over this fortress.'

The Flying Fortress was designed in 1934 as a private venture by the Boeing Company of Seattle. The prototype was far more advanced than any other bomber then flying.

Not only was the aircraft the first all-metal four-engine monoplane bomber, it was also considerably faster than the best US fighters. A limited order for 13 evaluation aircraft was made: their first use being to protect the US coastline from attack by an enemy fleet. However, air force commanders saw the Flying Fortress as an offensive weapon and around this bomber was evolved the doctrine of strategic bombing—the destruction of an enemy's factories and installations vital to his war economy. Some advocates went so far as to predict that a successful strategic bombing campaign could bring about an enemy's capitulation without the use of land armies.

The US plans involved daylight attack with bombers flying at very high altitudes—20,000ft or more—where they would be practically immune from fighter interception and above the accurate range of anti-aircraft guns. Targets would be pinpointed by the Norden precision bombsight (designed in 1932). so accurate that in the clear visibility of California or Texas an experienced bombardier could

△ B17s under construction at one of the Boeing Company's plants in Seattle, Washington.

▽ This B17B's bomb doors are open to receive its quota of 500lb HE bombs. Before being winched up into the aircraft, the bombs will be fused by ground-crew armorers. Standard bomb load was 6,000lb, and the B17B could operate a round trip of 1,300 miles with this weight. There was provision for an additional 8,000lb to be carried on under-wing shackles but the extra weight severely cut operational mileage and was not often used.

repeatedly drop bombs within a 100ft diameter on a practice range four miles (21,000ft) below. Other technical developments, making this form of aerial bombardment a practical proposition, were turbo-superchargers for the Flying Fortress's radial engines, giving the aircraft a maximum 300mph at 25,000ft; and advances in oxygen breathing equipment enabling aircrews to survive for many hours at high altitude. But these technical advances had not been used 'in anger'.

In April 1941, prior to the US entering the war, 20 Flying Fortress B17Cs were delivered to the Royal Air Force. The RAF had been engaged in daylight bombing operations since 1939, but the slow, unescorted British bombers were easy prey to the German fighters, and for that reason small forces of fast, light aircraft were employed on daylight raids. The vulnerability of bombers at that period was underlined by the heavy losses inflicted on the *Luftwaffe* day-bombers during the Battle of Britain.

With the Fortresses came a team of US specialists, quietly posted into Britain to advise the RAF on 'technical problems'. British pilots were soon impressed by the Fortress's impressive ability to climb into the sky quickly—35,000ft could be reached in 45 minutes. But the normal service ceiling was fixed at 33,300ft, still far above that of any other RAF bomber and a height that would put it beyond the range of German interceptor fighters. To the RAF it seemed possible that the Fortress could be used to bomb targets from the stratosphere, but US bombing policy was based on accurate attack from heights of about 25,000ft.

Operational debut

The RAF's No. 90 Squadron was given the job of flying the new Fortresses and it commenced training at airfields in Norfolk, moving finally to Polebrook, in the East Midlands, to make its operational debut. This came on 8 July when three Fortresses led by Wing Commander MacDougall set out to attack the dockyards at Wilhelmshaven. Only one claimed a successful attack, the others experiencing mechanical difficulties due to the sub-zero temperatures met during the high-altitude flight. In fact, of 24 operations the RAF flew during the summer of 1941, over half were abortive due to extreme cold. Bomb rack and machine-gun mechanisms became frozen up and the turbo-supercharger accessories regularly had icing troubles. At 35,000ft the temperature could be minus 50°F, causing discomfort to aircrews. They suffered, too, from all the unpleasant decompression symptoms after a high-altitude mission.

The Fortresses were usually immune from AA fire, but enemy fighters made several interceptions. The first followed an attack on Brest when one Fortress was attacked by three Me 109s. In the course of a 20-minute running fight, two air gunners were killed and another badly wounded, while the damage sustained by the bomber was so heavy that it crashed on landing. The second battle took place when three Fortresses were sent to bomb German warships in Oslo harbor. One bomber returned across the North Sea with only two engines functioning normally, but it crashed while attempting to land in Scotland. These incidents give an indication of the extremely sound construction of the aircraft.

By September 1941 the RAF decided that lack of success did not warrant further Fortress operations. No. 90 Squadron was disbanded, but the Americans had gleaned valuable information which enabled them to improve later B17 models. In spite of the aircraft's name, the armament of five .5in heavy machine-guns and one rifle-calibre weapon was found totally inadequate. All were hand held, so vibration, slip-stream pressure and low-temperature discomfort combined to make the gunners' task very difficult, and hits on an assailant highly unlikely. Furthermore, there was no tail gun-turret to protect the stern of the Fortress, which enemy fighters tended to attack.

Even before the RAF's abortive trials, the Boeing company had been working on an improved model, the B17E, which incorporated power-operated turrets and a tail-gun position. The whole rear fuselage had been redesigned with a completely new tail unit; and a large, distinctively shaped fin was fitted to counter the marked lack of directional stability of the original Fortress models at high altitude. The first of the new Fortresses was flown in September 1941 and the first service examples were reaching US squadrons when the Japanese blow fell on Pearl Harbor.

Of the 150 Fortresses that America began the war with, a third were with units in the Philippine Islands and Hawaii, and those few not destroyed on the ground during the early Japanese attacks were soon largely eliminated by the enemy's overwhelming forces. Nevertheless, the handful of Fortresses that survived to fight fared considerably better than those flown by the RAF the previous summer. Better bombing results were achieved because of the lower attack altitudes used, while in air combat the Fortresses were able to give a good account of themselves and survive against unfavorable odds. This was largely because most Japanese interceptors were equipped with rifle-calibre machine-guns —weapons which could not bring down these large bombers unless vital components were hit.

But vast distances had to be covered from the US bases in northern Australia and the New Hebrides, so it became apparent that the longer-ranged B24 Liberator (4,600 miles against the B17's 2,100) would be better suited to operations in this area. The B17 Fortress was gradually withdrawn from the Pacific war front to be used in Europe where its range was more than sufficient.

Birth of the 'Mighty 8th'

Soon after, on 1 July 1942, Flying Fortress 'Jarring Jenny' B17E, landed at Prestwick, Scotland, having flown the 3,000 miles from Maine via Greenland and Iceland. It was the first of hundreds of sister aircraft to be flown in in this way. The largest air striking force in history was established in Britain, in East Anglia. It was the birth of the mighty Eighth Air Force. The force began high-altitude daylight bombing operations in August 1942, and the first group of squadrons went to the original base at Polebrook and its satellite field at Grafton Underwood.

The B17F, standard model, supplied to the Eighth Air Force during late 1942, had 11 guns with two in each of the two power-operated turrets. Modifications made after arrival in Britain increased the Fortress's armament to 12 or 13 guns. The forward area was the least well defended and, because enemy fighters began to develop head-on attacks, the two or three additional guns were mounted in the nose of the aircraft.

Early American raids achieved small success. Bombing accuracy left much to be desired, but most missions were completed without loss. In contrast to the RAF's sorties, the numerically superior American force flew in close formation—'boxes'—where the combined fire of the many defensive machine-guns proved a dangerous obstacle to *Luftwaffe* fighters attempting to attack.

US Army

△ *Brand new, gleaming Flying Fortress B17Gs, newly arrived in Britain from US factories. Staked out in a parking bay, the bombers await issue to combat units, where squadron markings and identification symbols will be added. In the first aircraft, the 'chin' turret, holding two .5in machine-guns, can be seen. Through the perspex of the nose, the then secret Norden bomb sight is seen covered up.*
▽ *Clusters of incendiary bombs fall from Fortress B17Gs during a high-level operation over Europe. Following planes would drop high-explosive bombs on the fires created.*

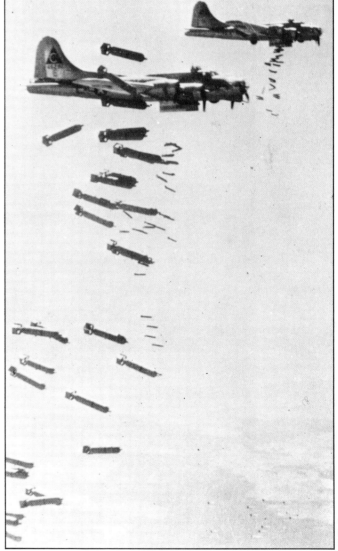

US Air Force

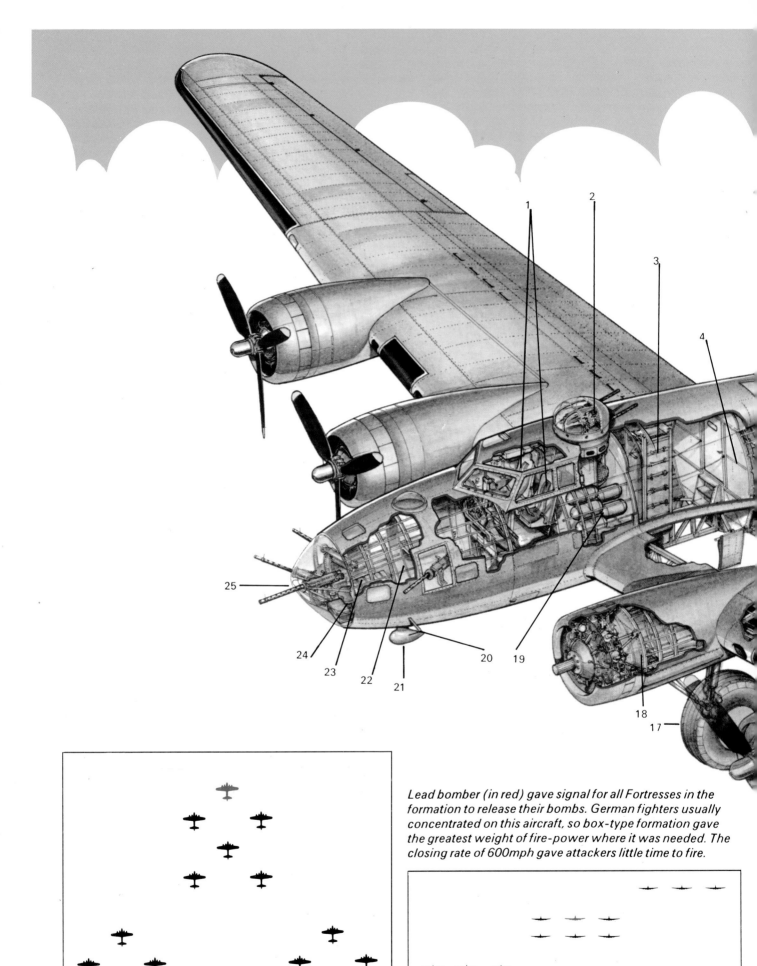

Lead bomber (in red) gave signal for all Fortresses in the formation to release their bombs. German fighters usually concentrated on this aircraft, so box-type formation gave the greatest weight of fire-power where it was needed. The closing rate of 600mph gave attackers little time to fire.

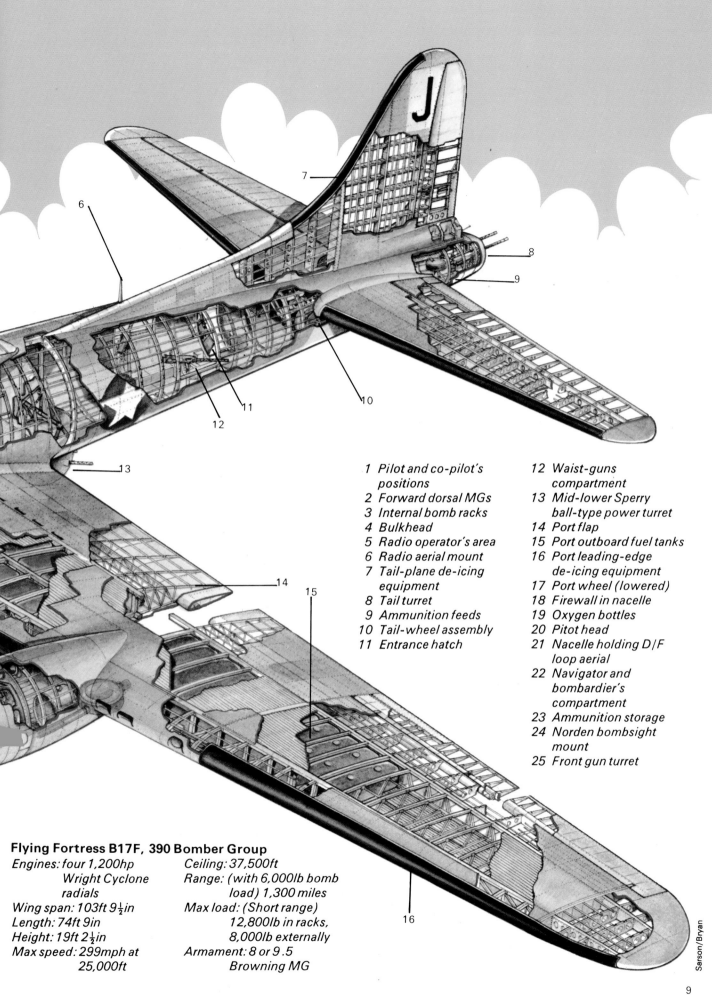

1 Pilot and co-pilot's positions
2 Forward dorsal MGs
3 Internal bomb racks
4 Bulkhead
5 Radio operator's area
6 Radio aerial mount
7 Tail-plane de-icing equipment
8 Tail turret
9 Ammunition feeds
10 Tail-wheel assembly
11 Entrance hatch
12 Waist-guns compartment
13 Mid-lower Sperry ball-type power turret
14 Port flap
15 Port outboard fuel tanks
16 Port leading-edge de-icing equipment
17 Port wheel (lowered)
18 Firewall in nacelle
19 Oxygen bottles
20 Pitot head
21 Nacelle holding D/F loop aerial
22 Navigator and bombardier's compartment
23 Ammunition storage
24 Norden bombsight mount
25 Front gun turret

Flying Fortress B17F, 390 Bomber Group
Engines: four 1,200hp Wright Cyclone radials
Wing span: 103ft 9½in
Length: 74ft 9in
Height: 19ft 2½in
Max speed: 299mph at 25,000ft
Ceiling: 37,500ft
Range: (with 6,000lb bomb load) 1,300 miles
Max load: (Short range) 12,800lb in racks, 8,000lb externally
Armament: 8 or 9.5 Browning MG

Sarson/Bryan

US Air Force

The technique of high-altitude daylight precision bombing was pioneered during the next six months by the B17s. The problems were many, a major handicap being the weather. Clear visibility was needed to make a precision bombing attack, but often after a three or four-hour flight over enemy territory the target was found to be obscured by cloud. In order to effectively saturate the small targets attacked, various formations were tried and eventually all aircraft dropped their bombs on the signal of the lead bomber; its bomb-aimer pin-pointed the target for everyone.

Some very successful strikes were made on targets along the seaboard of Occupied Europe. But on 27 January 1943 the Fortresses struck at Germany herself—with a raid on Wilhelmshaven. This new threat from the daylight sky—one which the Germans did not think could succeed—soon met with stiff opposition. Even so, the air gunners on the Fortresses usually shot down several of the attacking Messerschmitts and Focke-Wulfs, although their claims of aircraft destroyed were frequently exaggerated. In one notorious case, October 1942, trigger-happy gunners claimed 102 'kills' when precisely two German fighters were lost. This can be partly explained by the practice of awarding air gunners an air medal for their first victim.

A typical mission during this first year would entail a six to eight-hour flight to a target often 300 to 400 miles from base. As take-off would usually be soon after dawn, the 10-man crews were roused from their beds at least three hours beforehand for breakfast and briefing. Flying kit consisted of electrically heated suits and heavy fleece-lined clothing to prevent frostbite. A Fortress would take off from the runway every 30 seconds and the next two hours would be spent making wide orbits over the English countryside, at the same time gaining altitude and assembling into close formation. Once the formations were assembled into narrow bomber 'streams' they would head towards the enemy coast, climbing above 18,000ft in order to evade flak.

Few deep penetrations into Germany evaded fighter resistance and sometimes attacks would commence at the enemy coast and continue till the B17s recrossed it on the return flight. Large stocks of ammunition were carried and it was not unusual for the gunners on a single B17 to expend 6,000 rounds during a mission. On approach to the target individual formations would position themselves for the bomb run. While the Fortress could theoretically lift bomb loads of up to 17,600lb, its bomb-bay could only accommodate 4,000lb. Other bombs could be carried outside the bomb-bay, but the streamlining was so badly affected that the aircraft's range was reduced disastrously. The largest bomb carried was 2,000lb of high-explosive. Two of these, or four 1,000-pounders, formed the usual load carried by each bomber for an attack on an industrial target. After many hours on oxygen and exposed to the noise and cold, crews were always very fatigued. This type of flying was extremely demanding on human stamina—apart from the strain of combat.

Air battles of epic proportions occurred as the 8th USAF strove for daylight air supremacy, by aiming at such vital objectives as aircraft factories, oil refineries, submarine works, chemical plants and the ball-bearing industry. It was to the latter's heart at Schweinfurt, 400 miles from the Channel coast, that two of the most costly missions were run on 17 August and 14 October 1943. The first mission, combined with an attack on the Messerschmitt fighter plants at Regensburg and Wiener Neustadt, cost 60 out of 376 Fortresses and the same number also failed to return from the second raid of 291 B17s to Schweinfurt alone. Of those that did return another 17 were written off in crashed landings and 121 needed repairs, leaving just 93 aircraft undamaged. Worse still was the casualty list of 648 killed, wounded, and missing. Such crippling casualties, running at over 16 per cent of the force despatched, could not be sustained because of the loss of trained aircrews. It was obvious that long-range fighters would have to be employed if the US strategic bombing campaign was to continue.

From November 1943 onwards fighter support was available to 520 miles out; and the advent of the P51 Mustang eventually allowed US fighters to escort the

◁ *Tired but happy to be home safely. This B17G crew, led by Lt. John C. Stultz, 24, have brought their Fortress back to England from a raid on Frankfurt, Germany. Holdalls take chutes and portable gear. Crewman to Stoltz's left carries a flak-suit over his shoulder. Plane is already being fuelled for its next mission as a bowser tops tanks with 100 octane.*
▽ *A stick of 500lb HE bombs falling onto the harbor area of Naples during a raid by 100 Flying Fortresses. At least ten ships were hit, including two passenger liners. A group of bomb bursts can be seen in the sea by the harbor wall.*

heavy bombers all the way to the target. With this protection, the Fortresses—and the B24 Liberators, forming a third of the strike force from early 1944—flew with less harassment from enemy fighters. An early radar system (H2S) gave them the ability to strike from above cloud-base. But increasingly powerful German AA weapons took a heavy toll of the American bombers during the last year of the war. At some targets, notably the vital synthetic oil plants at Ploesti, as many as 500 heavy guns were deployed to hurl fearful barrages at the close formations. Again the Fortress's remarkable ability to sustain severe damage and still fly on enabled many aircraft to return to friendly territory. On Schweinfurt raids some crippled B17s landed in Switzerland and Sweden.

By May 1945 the USAF had 108 Fortress squadrons in the UK and 24 in Italy (over 1,200 aircraft), while the RAF had eight in Coastal Command for meteorological and anti-submarine work and two special radio counter-measures units in Bomber Command to support its night bombers. Even the Germans had thought highly of the aircraft and used several captured examples for clandestine operations, chiefly to convey agents behind the Allied lines.

Crews' close-knit spirit

The crews of B17s had the same close-knit spirit as a veteran infantry squad. Each aircraft's 10 men had his specialization, there being a pilot, co-pilot, navigator, flight engineer, wireless operator, bomb-aimer, belly gunner (in the aptly-named 'morgue'—the cramped belly turret), two waist gunners, and a tail gunner—the loneliest man of all. And some air crew completed as many as 120 missions. There were numerous instances of crewmen giving up their parachutes to wounded comrades. Pilots showed extraordinary devotion, doing their utmost to nurse crippled 'Forts' home after all other crewmen had jumped. Another facet of the high morale was an addiction to 'nose art'—painting aircraft nicknames and emblems, including a high proportion of naked and semi-naked females.

Pilots found it an easy aircraft to fly, docile, positive in control and extremely stable. It was this stability that made the Fortress such a good 'bombing platform', essential for accurate use of the precision bomb-sight at 25,000ft. The basic soundness of the aircraft's aerodynamics explains how Fortresses could and did return over many hundreds of miles with incredible battle damage. Large parts of wings, fuselage and tail could be shot away—there were occasions when complete tail stabilizers were severed—but still the aircraft would make safe landings. One or two engines were often put out of action and it was not unknown for a Fortress to get home with only one of the four functioning. In April 1944 Fortress 'Bertie Lee' came back from a 1,200-mile flight with burning incendiaries in a jammed bomb-bay as well as a shattered cockpit area with no working flaps or undercarriage.

Almost 5,000 Fortresses out of 13,000 built were lost through accident or combat. The greater proportion of these went down during the great air battles over north-west Europe in 1943 and 1944. It was these actions—without parallel in their scope and intensity—that brought the B17 its fame. Not once during the period when the Fortress formations battled alone through the stratosphere to reach their objectives was a mission turned back by enemy action.

Roger A. Freeman

A US bombardier using the Norden bombsight in the nose of a B17. This sight give amazing accuracy in the hands of a competent man, enabling him to place his bombs within yards of a target from four miles high.

NORDEN BOMBSIGHT

Top-secret for years, a wonder-sight with 'pickle barrel' accuracy. But later matched by a not-so-lauded RAF model

With flak bursting off-target, B24 Liberators bomb the Concordia Vega oil refinery at Ploesti, Rumania, on 31 May 1944. This raid, by the 15th USAAF, was by 460 heavy bombers as part of a concentrated offensive against German oil plants.

When the highly trained young bomber crews of the United States 8th Air Force began arriving in England in the summer of 1942 they brought with them an unshakeable faith in the concept of high-altitude daylight strategic bombing. Battle-hardened veterans of the RAF shook their heads in disbelief. The British had been forced to abandon daylight bombing early in the war when formations were cut to pieces by German fighters. The *Luftwaffe* learnt a similarly expensive lesson during the Battle of Britain. Night raids certainly reduced bomber losses to manageable proportions, but accuracy left a lot to be desired, even when attacks were carried out at altitudes of below 10,000ft. As British bomber strength grew so the practice of area bombing was born—blanketing whole sections of a city with bombs, so that high-precision aiming was not necessary.

Only by sending out bombers in daylight, the Americans asserted, was it possible to pin-point the important targets —factories and military installations. And they planned to go in at over 20,000ft, where they would be less vulnerable to AA fire.

The vital factor upon which this revolutionary strategy depended was the top-secret Norden bombsight. Without this complex device it would have been ridiculous to even consider precision bombing from four miles high, with the additional problems posed by cross winds and the need to take evasive action in the face of flak and defending fighters.

Three years later, in the spring of 1945, Germany lay in ruins. From Kiel in the north to Munich in the south her cities had been reduced to heaps of rubble. As the war neared its end, the RAF were regularly sending out 1,000-strong raids. There can be no doubt of the efficiency with which the British obliterated Hamburg, Cologne, Dresden and a dozen other cities—including, eventually, Berlin itself. But when Albert Speer, the Nazi Armaments and War Production Minister, was interrogated after the war he affirmed that the mass daylight attacks were the most effective in weakening the German war effort because they 'were based upon economic considerations and inflicted heavy damage on precise targets'. It was the Norden bombsight which made this vital American contribution to the Allied victory possible.

The origins of this piece of equipment can be traced back to 1921, when the US Navy asked consulting engineer Carl L. Norden, a Dutch-born authority on gyroscopes, to devise a gyro-stabilized base for their existing Mark 3 bombsight so that it could be used from high altitude.

The device that Norden evolved worked perfectly well as long as the target was stationary. Unfortunately, enemy ships are rarely obliging enough to remain at anchor when attacked. The Navy accordingly asked for a more refined bombsight still. One that could be used against moving targets.

This was a much more complicated problem than just providing a stabilizer for an existing sight. Norden enlisted the services of an engineer, Theodore Harold Barth, and an officer from the US Navy Bureau of Ordnance, Lieutenant-Commander Frederick I. Entwhistle, and set to work.

Early beginnings

The Mark 11 gyro-optical sight was developed in 1924. It incorporated a timing device to indicate the correct moment for bomb release. But this was only a beginning. And the Mark 11 sight was not ready for testing at the Naval Proving Ground, Dahlgren, Virginia until 1928. It was installed in a Martin bomber and a Naval flier, J. J. Ballentine, was detailed to make the first practice drop using the new sight. Unfortunately, no allowance had been made for the very low temperatures experienced at altitude. The day of the test was particularly cold. The components of the delicate sight had been toleranced in the warmth of the laboratory. When Ballentine began his run he found that the device was completely frozen up. To an experienced experimental flier like Ballentine, test bombing runs were routine and he decided not to disappoint Carl Norden, who was watching on the ground. He made the drop, with excellent results—by rule of thumb!

Ballentine landed and climbed cheerfully from the bomber, only to be met by a downcast Carl Norden: 'Bally, you don't have to tell me. The sight didn't work. You dropped those bombs by eye!'

Norden did not admit defeat easily, however, and he soon overcame the inevitable problems of a new piece of complicated equipment. In 1929 the Mark 11 sight was yielding 50 per cent better results than the old Mark 3 and the Navy ordered 80 examples.

Despite the accuracy attainable with the Mark 11 the Navy was not happy with the complexity of the instrument and there were misgivings about its operational requirements. The timing mechanism required the aircraft's speed during a bomb run to be established at a substantial distance from the target and accurately maintained throughout a long approach. In battle, a bomber would be a sitting duck for defending fighters and AA fire whilst on the run-up, and even without these hazards the pilot's skill would be at a premium to keep to a constant speed and hold the plane absolutely level.

Carl Norden went back to work. A new company— Carl L. Norden Inc.—was founded in New York City in 1928. By 1931 another new bombsight was ready—the famous Mark 15. With this instrument the closing speed of the attack could be established at any time during the

run-up and although a long steady approach was still necessary, a fixed speed and altitude had only to be maintained for 15 or 20 seconds.

The Mark 15 was tested against the hulk of the old heavy cruiser *Pittsburgh* in 1931 and the results so impressed the US Army that they placed an order for the new sight on top of what the Navy needed.

One more refinement was necessary before the Mark 15 became the war-winner of 1941/45. No pilot, however skilful, can fly with complete accuracy because he is constantly correcting for drift, checking his altitude, adjusting his airspeed and making innumerable minor alterations to his control settings. Together, these fluctuations have an adverse effect on bombing accuracy, and the greater the altitude from which the bombs are dropped, the wider the error becomes by the time they hit the ground.

To ensure the smoothest possible flying conditions on a bombing run, Norden devised a gyro-stabilized automatic pilot, known as Stabilized Bombing Approach Equipment (SBAE) to the Navy and Automatic Flight Control Equipment (AFCE) to the Army. This took over control of the aircraft on the run-in and eliminated the roughness of manual flying. It was now possible for any service aircrew to bomb with an accuracy that only the specialists at the Naval proving ground had been able to achieve before. From four miles above the dry lake at Muroc, California, Army fliers found that they were consistently dropping their bombs within 50ft of a practice target. These feats were enthusiastically referred to as 'pickle-barrel accuracy', and as a result American bomber crews acquired a reputation for being able to lob a bomb into a pickle-barrel from 20,000ft.

The final form

In its final form the Norden bombsight weighed 45lb and incorporated over 2,000 components. The stabilizer consisted of two electric gyros, one of which was set up to detect deviation from the aircraft's set course (the directional gyro), whilst the other registered any tendency to either roll or to nose-up or nose-down (the flight gyro). The sight was mounted on top of the stabilizer and was fitted with a 2.5 power telescope driven by a variable speed electric motor; a computer consisting of innumerable cams, gears, prisms, lenses and mirrors; and a gyro to hold the sight stable.

Before the Norden sight could be used the bombardier had to feed certain basic data into its computer. From pre-calculated tables he would get the time the bombs would take to fall (based on the speed and altitude scheduled for the run-in), and the distance behind the plane that the bombs would hit the ground (known as the trail). About five minutes out from the target the plane's drift was checked to find out if there was a cross wind. This factor had also to be fed into the computer. As the target came into view the bombardier trained the telescope on it and adjusted the telescope drive so that the instrument maintained its alignment with the objective.

When the clutches that controlled the bombsight were operated to activate the instrument, the stabilizer-controlled auto-pilot system immediately cut in. The directional gyro and the flight gyro both had electrical brushes fitted to them. If the plane moved off course, the gyro retained its orientation and consequently moved inside its housing. The brushes then made contact with solenoids that engaged electric servo motors which in turn operated the control

Official USAF Photo

"It's Cadet Schmaltz, sir – he's hopeless!"

Flight

Real John Wayne stuff as gun-toting aircrew of the USAAF escort their Norden bombsight to the bomber. Censorship has obliterated the flat perspex bomb-aimer's panel. The aircraft is a Douglas B18A, military version of the DC2.

surfaces and rectified the deviation. There was normally a link between the rudder and aileron servo motors to give bank in turns, but a special switch could be thrown that left all directional control to the rudder and eliminated bank.

The bombardier was able to manipulate the stabilizer to take evasive action in heavy flak, although there were mechanical stops in the auto-pilot that made steep banks impossible. Once the bomb run proper began, however, the plane was held rigidly straight and level by the stabilizer. The telescope tracked the target in until it reached the critical dropping angle, when the bombs were released automatically.

The complex computer made it possible to allow for any drift affecting the plane, as well as influencing the bombs during their fall. Moving targets could be hit as easily as stationary ones, since it did not matter if any apparent movement of the objective relative to the bomber was caused by a cross wind or by the mobility of the target.

There was only one serious fault with the Norden bombsight. It could not be used below 1,800ft. Attempts to adapt it for low-level use failed. This meant that it was of limited value to the Navy, who were principally required to undertake low-level strikes and dive bombing. When production really began to gather momentum in 1940 under the spur of an escalating European war, it was to the Army that most Norden sights were sent. The B17 Flying Fortress, the B24 Liberator, the B25 Mitchell, the B26 Marauder and the A20 Havoc were among the aircraft into which the sight was to be fitted. The small numbers sent to the Navy were earmarked for the PBM Mariner, PBY Catalina, PB4Y Liberator, TBD Devastator and the TBF Avenger.

A new Naval ordnance plant was set up at Indianapolis to augment production from Norden's New York factory and an output of 800 bomb-sights a month was envisaged at the beginning of 1941. The Japanese attack on Pearl Harbor in December 1941 meant a drastic upgrading of that figure. Extra production sites had to be found, and contracts were placed with commercial firms that had suitable manufacturing facilities. Towards the end of 1943 output reached almost 2,000 sights a month.

Blanket security surrounded the Mark 15 bombsights when they entered service. They were never left unattended in aircraft. After every mission they were unshipped for storage in air-conditioned dust-proof vaults surrounded by high barbed-wire fences under constant guard. When a sight was needed for action it was carried to the aircraft by two armed servicemen. The canvas cover shrouding the device was not removed until the bomber was airborne.

On its very first missions from England in the summer of

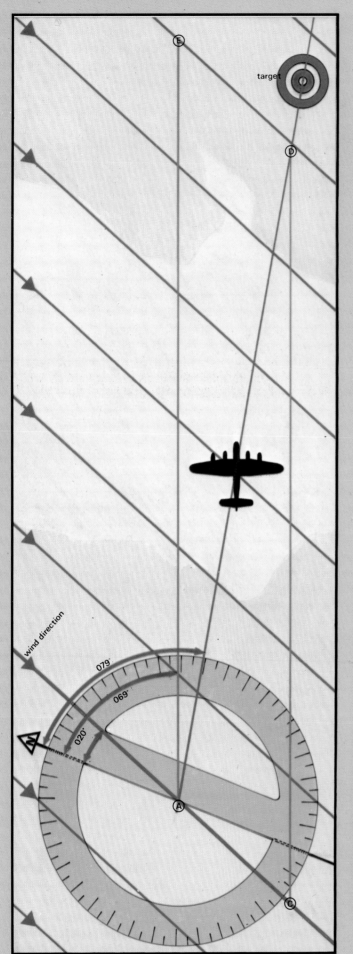

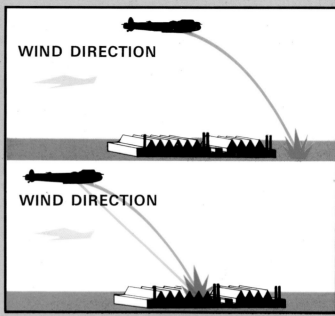

WIND DIRECTION

WIND DIRECTION

△ *A bomb from an aircraft right above a target will miss. When fed with the ballistic data, altitude, speed, drift angle, the Norden automatically released the bomb when the target reached the critical angle in the sight.*

◁ *Wind speed and direction affect an aircraft's movement over the ground. On the map the bomber is on track from A to target. Wind (a moving air-mass) from 020° at 40mph (A-C) will take the aircraft away from target and reduce its speed over the ground to 175mph(A-D) even though its air-speed indicator will show 200mph. To reach the target the bomber must head on a compass course of 069° (A-E).*

▽ *The navigator found his drift with a drift-sight. When markings on the ground ran parallel to wires in the sight the angle of drift was read from the scale on the rim. Angle of drift is the angle at which the aircraft is pointed in comparison with its track over the ground.*

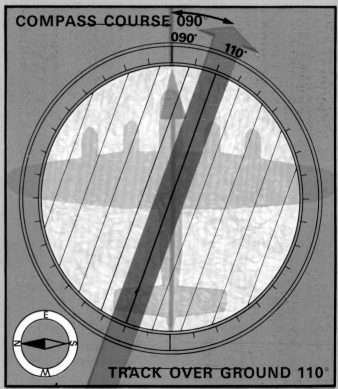

COMPASS COURSE 090°

TRACK OVER GROUND 110°

Davis & Harrison VP Ltd

1942 the US 8th Air Force was detailed to attack pin-point targets such as the locomotive workshops at Rouen marshalling yards, the *Luftwaffe* servicing base at Romilly-sur-Seine, and the submarine pens at St. Nazaire, Brest and Lorient, using the Norden sight to bomb from four miles up.

The British-based Fortress outfits soon discovered that allowing each plane in a squadron to maneuver independently to drop its bombs was likely to break up the defensive formation intended to give American air gunners maximum mutual protection from German fighters—as well as increasing the risk of collisions and creating general confusion. Colonel Curtis Le May, commander of the 305th Bomb Group, decided that only the lead ship in each formation should line up on the target, the rest of the bombers unloading when they saw their leader drop. The best crews and the most skilled bombardiers were assigned to fly in the lead planes.

This new idea worked well, and reduced the likelihood of poor bombing by inexperienced crews, such as occurred on 5 September 1942 when 140 French civilians died during a raid on the Rouen marshalling yards as a result of bombs falling wide of the target. This kind of incident gave the German propaganda ministry a sturdy stick with which to beat the Allies.

Bombing accuracy was computed by assessing the proportion of hits falling within 1,000ft and 2,000ft circles about an MPI (mean point of impact). To achieve a perfect strike, a group would have to unload all its bombs within the 1,000ft circle. By the spring of 1943 some impressive results were being recorded. Over Vegesack on 18 March, for instance, the 305th Group dropped 76 per cent of its load within the 1,000ft ring. On this raid the 8th Air Force earned its first Congressional Medal of Honor, awarded to 1st Lieutenant Jack Mathis—lead bombardier of the 359th Squadron. Flying at 24,000ft with only a minute to go before reaching the dropping point, Mathis was peering intently through his Norden sight when an AA shell exploded just to the right of the B17's nose. Fragments shattered the plexiglass and hurled Mathis 9ft to the back of the compartment, almost severing his right arm and inflicting mortal wounds to his body. He somehow managed to drag himself back to his sight and released the bombs—the signal for the rest of the squadron to unload—but as he reached for the switch that closed the bomb bay doors he collapsed and died.

First time out for AFCE

The Vegesack mission was also the first raid on which the AFCE (automatic flight control equipment) had successfully been employed. Early difficulties with this device were overcome by judicious modifications and most group lead bombers subsequently carried AFCE. But crews never regarded it as infallible despite its pre-war use on long-distance seaplane flights from San Diego to the Panama Canal Zone and from San Francisco to Honolulu.

In the Pacific, the B24 Liberators of the 7th Air Force were carrying out missions involving nearly 3,000 miles of trans-ocean flying, with targets that were frequently no bigger than a radio station, such as the one on Rongelap in the Marshall Islands that was housed in a building only 35ft by 125ft. On that occasion the B24s went in at 3,500ft and used only 100lb bombs—relying on the accuracy of their Norden bombsights to accomplish the destruction of the Japanese communications center. During the Marshalls campaign of early 1944 the 7th Air Force claimed that 92 per cent of its bombs landed on the selected targets.

Over northern Europe the Americans encountered a problem. Mission after mission was scrapped or aborted as successive weather fronts from the Atlantic moved across the British Isles and heavy cloud obscured the sky. Not even the Norden bombsight could overcome this problem. The only answer was radar.

In such remote theaters of war as China and the Aleutians the Norden revolutionized aerial bombardment. When American forces occupied Kiska and Attu islands at the western end of the Aleutian chain in 1943 they found the Japanese installations in ruins as a result of accurate bombing. The defenders were forced to take refuge in caves. At Kiska, US bombers went over at 18,000ft.

Even from this altitude they succeeded in rendering the Japanese runway unusable and destroyed an oil dump, knocking out as well most of the AA gun emplacements and sinking shipping in the harbor.

'Blue Ox' proves itself

Conditions in China posed particular problems for high-altitude bomber crews. Targets were usually small and widely dispersed. The weather was anything but helpful, with heavy cloud, buffeting winds that gusted at up to 100mph, tropical heat at ground level, and sub-zero temperatures four miles high. The Norden sight, by now popularly known to American fliers as the 'blue ox', proved equal to all the demands made on it.

By mid-1943 American bombers based in England were thrusting deep into the Reich itself. In July the Continental Gumi-Weke factory at Hanover was attacked by B17s that in some cases went in at heights of over 30,000ft but bombed with such accuracy that 21 direct hits were scored—slashing production of tyres and synthetic rubber at the plant by almost 25 per cent for many weeks to come. Orders for the raid on the Messerschmitt factory at Regensburg on 17 August specified bombing heights of only 17,000 to 19,000ft to ensure maximum accuracy. The 390th Bombardment Group dropped 58 per cent of their bombs within 1,000ft of the aiming point and 94 per cent within 2,000ft, leaving the target hidden beneath a pall of smoke and flames. Most of the fuselage jigs for the new Messerschmitt 262 jet fighter were destroyed by this strike.

Still lower bombing altitudes of 11,000 to 13,000ft were stipulated for a raid on the Focke-Wulf factory at Marienburg during October. The AA defenses were known to be weak here. Results were again good, with 58 per cent within 1,000ft of the aiming point and 83 per cent inside the 2,000ft circle.

Dense cloud severely restricted American air operations over Europe during the winter of 1943-44. Those bomber missions that were carried out depended heavily on the use of pathfinder aircraft equipped with radar. A brief break in the weather on 11 January allowed 650 bombers to be sent to the Brunswick area, where the Messerschmitt 110 factory at Waggum was subjected to concentrated visual bombing. The 94th Bombardment Group's 20 B17s had 73 per cent of their bombs land within 1,000ft of the aiming point and not one of them beyond 2,000ft.

Towards the end of February the skies began to clear and the Norden bombsight came into its own again, with objectives as far afield as Berlin appearing regularly on target schedules from early March.

The Allied invasion of Europe in June 1944 meant the

diversion of Anglo-American air power to tactical targets in support of the armies battling their way ashore in Normandy. US heavy bombers used their Nordens to good effect in attacks on fortifications, roads, railways, and the launching sites from which the Nazis were directing pilotless flying bombs (V1s) and giant rocket projectiles (V2s) against England.

By April 1945 Germany was on the point of total collapse and the European war was drawing rapidly to its close. US 8th Air Force B24s of the crack 467th Group set a new standard for precision bombing. Detailed to destroy a German battery still holding out at Pointe de Grave, on the west coast of France, the three Liberator squadrons scored a 100 per cent strike—every bomb within 1,000ft of the MPI. Half of these were within 500ft.

Norden sights were inevitably captured by the Germans and the Japanese. Early in the Pacific war it had been possible to send a special US Navy recovery team to a coral atoll south of Hawaii just to salvage a Catalina flying boat—sunk with a Mark 15 sight installed. The plane was dragged up with grappling hooks, the sight was systematically smashed, and the wreckage returned to the sea bed. By the end of 1943, however, the Americans were losing as many as 60 four-engined bombers on a single mission over Europe, and the Norden sight was standard equipment in B17s and B24s.

The complexity of the Norden was such that American experts believed the Germans would need two years at least to unravel its mysteries and set up production facilities for manufacturing a copy.

In fact the *Luftwaffe* never developed a long-range high-altitude strategic bomber force, and consequently had no real need for a sight like the Norden. At the beginning of World War II the German air force had the fully automatic, electrically-driven Goerz release (G-A) sight. This was fitted with a heating device for use in cold climates or at high altitude and could drop a stick of bombs across a

target from any chosen point.

In the summer of 1940 the standard sight used by German twin-engined bombers was the pendulum-stabilized LOTFE 7B, but this was being replaced during the Battle of Britain by the 7C, which had a pendulum-controlled gyroscope. All 7B sights were gradually returned to the Zeiss factory at Jena for modifying to 7C standard. The appearance of this new aid to bombing caused mild con-

Official USAF Photo

1 *Over 40 per cent of all Luftwaffe Me 109Gs were produced at Messerschmitt's main factory at Augsburg, situated in a bend of the Danube near the Austrian border.*
2 *On 17 August 1943, B17s struck, their Norden sights placing the bombs where they would do the most damage. The aircraft then flew on to North Africa.*
3 *The Norden bombsight installed.*
4 *A low-level target not suitable for the high-level Norden. The Moehne Dam, hit by the RAF's 617 Sqdn (the 'Dam Busters') on 17 May 1943.*
5 *The RAF's Mk XIVA, also used by 617 Sqdn. It could be operated even if the bomber was taking evasive action. Its operational ceiling was 25,000ft.*

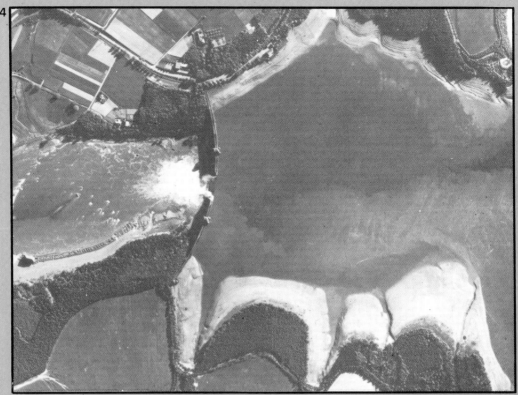

Imperial War Museum

W. Howes

soon as the nights became long enough for bomber operations in the autumn of 1940.

Early in 1945 a Zeiss bombsight fell into Allied hands. The influence of the Norden was evident. This electrically and mechanically operated device apparently controlled the plane during a bombing run, but in the absence of any German strategic bombing capability it must have been of small value to the *Luftwaffe*.

The RAF used a similar bombsight to the Norden, known as the Mark III SABS (Stabilized Automatic Bombsight). This was developed between 1938-41 but was eventually used almost exclusively by No 617 Squadron (the famous 'Dam Busters'), who were reserved for special precision bombing missions after their Lancasters were equipped with the Mark IIA sight during the latter part of 1943.

The area bombing technique favored by the RAF did not require a precision sight and could be adequately undertaken with the British Mark XIV bombsight, a continuously-set vector sight with a remotely stowed mechanical computer that relayed the drift angle and bombing angle to a sighting head in front of the bombardier. The operational limits of the Mark XIV were 1,000 to 20,000ft and 120 to 300mph, but wind speed and direction had to be accurately known as these factors were fed into the computer and incorrect data resulted in substantial errors. Bombsights based on the tachometric principle (such as the British Mark IIA) compute wind velocity and direction automatically during the aiming process.

The Mark XIVA represented a more refined development of the vector-type bomb-sight and was widely used by the RAF in both Bomber and Coastal Commands. It embodied a barometric altimeter, which imposed a ceiling of 25,000ft on its use, and there was still the problem of ensuring that wind speed and direction were correctly assessed, but the Mark XIVA could be operated even if a bomber was banking to avoid flak or fighters, whereas

sternation in Britain. Rumors of it reached the Prime Minister's office in July 1940 and Winston Churchill demanded a report on a 7C found in a crashed Heinkel 111. Experts at the Royal Aeronautical Establishment, Farnborough, Hampshire, rebuilt the badly damaged sight and reported unfavorably upon it because the gyroscope proved uncontrollable. Nevertheless, the Zeiss works was listed as a primary target for RAF Bomber Command as

Official USAF Photo

△ *The official caption to this photograph says one wing of this B17 over Berlin is on fire. But the shape, color and turbulence of the 'smoke' suggests that it is no more than a condensation trail caused by expanding exhaust gases from the bomber's engines.*

◁ *A column of smoke, thousands of feet high, as evidenced by its shadow on the ground, rises from the site of an oil refinery at Dortmund, Germany. Using the Norden bombsight, US 8th Air Force B17 Fortresses hit the target fair and square. Two strings of bombs can be seen on their way, with white markers streaming down for following bombers. Old bomb craters pock-mark the ground from previous raids.*

the Mark 11A SABS demanded a straight and level bombing run of at least 20 seconds.

No 9 Squadron, RAF, became a similar 'special mission' unit to No 617, but No 9's Lancasters used Mark XIVA sights. It was found that No 617's bombing was marginally more accurate than No 9's, but the SABS sight had to be set up by an expert from the Royal Aeronautical Establishment, needed very skilled bombardiers to operate it efficiently, and could really only be employed on lightly defended targets if prohibitive losses in highly trained crews were not to be suffered. Evasive action on the last stages of the bombing run was not possible. The SABS sight could be used from 5,000 to 25,000ft, but was not tropicalized for hot climates and had limited value for night bombing. But it was more accurate than the Mark XIVA against moving targets taking little or no evasive action.

Comparative tests between the Norden and the Mark IIA carried out by RAF Group Captain Leonard Cheshire indicated that the Mark IIA required a shorter run-in time to the target and the RAF assessors expressed a preference for the British sight which they considered more efficient than its American counterpart.

In the Pacific the Norden sight was to play a vital part in the closing stages of the war against Japan. With US forces established on the Mariana Islands in mid-1944, the giant new B29 Superfortress bombers, equipped with M-series sights, were within comfortable striking distance of the Japanese homeland and an intensive bombing offensive began to gather momentum.

The B29s were bombing from as much as 30,000ft and at that height over Japan strong jet-stream winds blowing at 120 knots seriously affected bombing accuracy. Eventually the B29s were stripped of their guns and sent in at night with incendiaries to burn-out the highly inflammable Japanese cities.

Into 500ft circle from 30,000ft

One Superfortress outfit became a specially trained elite force. The 509th Composite Group of the 315th Bombardment Wing had been activated at Wendover Army Air Field, Utah, in December 1944. Their planes were specially prepared B29s, without gun turrets, that were maintained to meticulous engineering standards (the unit never lost a single Superfortress either in training or in actual combat).

Under their commanding officer, Colonel Paul W. Tibbets Jr., the bombardiers of the 509th learnt how to use their Nordens to drop their bombs within a 500ft circle from 30,000ft.

After final training in Cuba the 509th moved to Tinian in May and June 1945. The activities of this top-secret group were a mystery even to other B29 units in the Marianas. There was a good reason for the stringent security. On 6 August one of the 509th Group's special B29s dropped the first atomic bomb on Hiroshima from an altitude of 31,600ft. Three days later the Group dropped a second nuclear weapon on Nagasaki. Conditions were so bad that it had been decided to bomb by radar, ignoring orders specifying a visual drop. The big Boeing was brought in blind and on instruments, but just seconds before reaching the release point the clouds opened up. Control was instantly handed over to the bombardier, who unleashed the massive bomb that seconds later devastated the heart of Nagasaki.

Within days of the second nuclear strike Japan sued for peace. The Norden bombsight had played a vital role in the two decisive bombing missions that effectively ended World War II. Production of the M-series sight finally ceased in September 1945, 43,292 having been manufactured at a cost of $500,000,000. All but 6,434 of them went to the Army.

Not until 1955 was the security blanket on the famous Norden sight at last lifted. By then it had been superseded by later developments and Carl Norden was allowed to take out a patent on his invention—something that had been impossible for him to do during the secrecy of the war years, although the design had been filed with the US Patent Office way back in 1930. Anyone could now buy a copy of the plans for a mere 25 cents. It was not long before stores selling government surplus goods were offering actual Norden bombsights for just $50!

Gary Craig

MAILLY-LE-CAMP

'If you're going to die—die like a man!' What went wrong as the German night-fighters struck?

'Why can't we go in and bomb now?' called a plaintive Canadian voice. 'Dry your bloody tears!' came the anonymous reply. It was a unique and unholy RAF 'flap' during a precision raid on Occupied France in 1944.

While Bomber Command's contribution to World War II is usually remembered for its sustained night bombing offensive against the industrial heartland of Germany, there was a six-month period in the middle of 1944—the year of the Allied invasion of Europe—when Bomber Command's main role was to bomb purely military targets. Many feared that the bombers could not yet hit such small targets without killing many civilians in German-occupied countries, but these raids achieved unexpectedly brilliant results.

High on the target list allocated to Bomber Command in preparation for D-day stood the name of Mailly-le-Camp. The village of Mailly is situated 80 miles east of Paris, between the towns of Troyes and Châlons-sur-Marne. At one

end of the village was a former French Army camp with barrack buildings, offices, workshops and a large armored-vehicle exercise area. This large camp was known to be used by the Germans for the training and reinforcement of front-line *Panzer* units and was believed to hold at least 10,000 men.

On 3 May Air Chief Marshal Sir Arthur T. Harris, C-in-C, Bomber Command, decided that conditions were ripe for an attack on Mailly-le-Camp during the coming night of a threequarters moon. Cloudless conditions were forecast for northern France. Harris decided that only two of his six bomber groups would carry out the raid—Nos 1 and 5 Groups, both equipped with the Lancaster, the best heavy bomber in service at that time. One of 5 Group's units was No. 617 Squadron, the famous 'Dambusters', led by 27-year-old Wing Commander Geoffrey Leonard Cheshire, subsequently awarded the VC for his development and

Middlebrook Collection

A four-engined Avro Lancaster of RAF Bomber Command makes a low pass over a war-time airfield.
◁▽ *Bomb-Aimer Flt. Sgt. Patfield, in a Lancaster of 61 Sqdn, took this photograph of another aircraft on its bombing run over Mailly on 4/5 May 1944. Towering columns of smoke rise from HE hits. Some 1,500 tons of bombs were dropped and over 160 buildings were destroyed or damaged, together with over a hundred vehicles, including tanks.*

Quotations from Crown copyright records in the Public Record Office appear by permission of the Controller of HM Stationary Office. Extracts from Squadron Operational Record Books are from PRO AIR 27/688 (83 Sqdn.) and AIR 27/1931 (467 Sqdn.). German material was provided by Bundesarchiv, Koblenz. Map details come from survivors of shot-down bombers and from material provided by the Air Historical Branch (particularly by Mr. D. C. Bateman) and the Commonwealth War Graves Commission.

Imperial War Museum

execution of pin-point, low-level marking. No. 1 Group usually operated with the main strength of Bomber Command and had no specialist squadrons.

The plan of attack had two basic requirements. First, placing of target markers and subsequent bombing had to be extremely accurate so that the village should not be hit. Secondly, the attack had to develop quickly before the Germans could take cover in their air raid shelters and before German night fighters could arrive on the scene. These two requirements were not easily satisfied, but a plan was evolved after several hours of consultation between Bomber Command staff officers and the two Groups concerned.

The attack was timed to open at midnight, one minute after the traditional time for all soldiers to return to camp. Three 'Aiming Points' were chosen—one at each end of the main group of barrack buildings and a third at the tank workshops some distance away. W/Cdr. Cheshire was to lead four Mosquito light bombers to place markers, from a low-level, on the first of these Aiming Points. Experienced Pathfinder crews from Nos 83 and 97 Squadrons would illuminate the area with flares to assist the Mosquito crews.

The first Aiming Point was then to be bombed by 140 Lancasters of 5 Group. Ten minutes later Cheshire's Mosquitos were to mark the other end of the barracks for the second wave—140 Lancasters of 1 Group. While these two attacks were in progress, crews of 1 Group's new marker unit would mark the tank-repair workshops and 30 more 1 Group Lancasters would bomb that target. Only 4,000lb 'blockbusters' and 500lb HE bombs were to be dropped—no incendiaries. Each Lancaster carried one 'blockbuster' and 15 or 16 500lb bombs.

Really accurate bombing of Mailly-le-Camp demanded strict control. Cheshire was designated 'Marker Leader' to ensure that the markers fell into the camp and not the village. Wing Commander L. C. Deane of 83 Squadron was to be the 'Main Force Controller' and would call in the bombers only when Cheshire was satisfied with the marking. Another 83 Sqdn. pilot, Squadron Leader E. N. M. Sparks, would act as 'Deputy Controller' if Deane was shot down or had to turn back with mechanical trouble. Although the attack was planned to last 29 minutes the timetable could be altered by Cheshire and Deane.

Soon after 2200 on 4 May, 346 heavily laden Lancasters started taking off from their Lincolnshire airfields. The weather was fine, the visibility clear, and there were no take-off accidents. Climbing steadily, the bombers flew almost due south to the first turning point at Reading and then SE over Beachy Head and across the Channel to Dieppe. The French coast was crossed at 12,000ft, the

WAITING LANCASTER AND BOMB-TROLLEY WITH TALLBOY BOMB

Peter Sarson/Tony Bryan

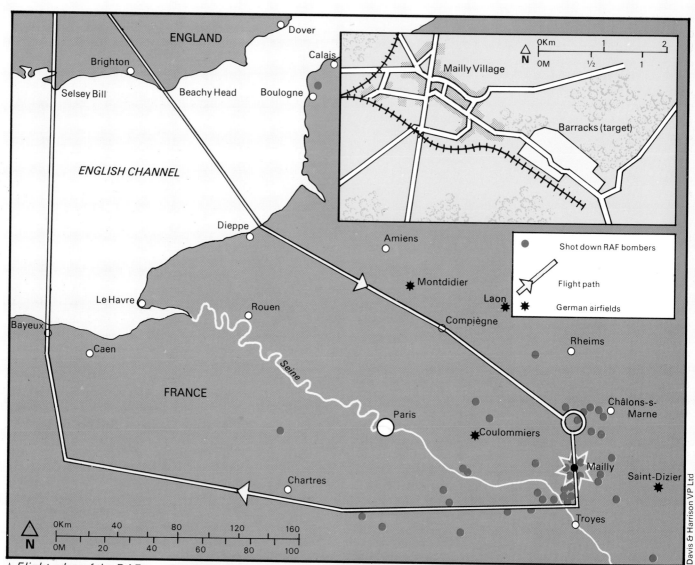

Mailly Village

0 Km 1 2
0 M ½ 1
N

Barracks (target)

Shot down RAF bombers
Flight path
German airfields

ENGLAND
Dover
Brighton
Calais
Selsey Bill
Beachy Head
Boulogne

ENGLISH CHANNEL

Dieppe
Amiens
Montdidier
Laon
Le Havre
Rouen
Compiègne
Rheims
Bayeux
Caen
Seine
Châlons-s-Marne
FRANCE
Paris
Coulommiers
Chartres
Mailly
Saint-Dizier
Troyes

0 Km 40 80 120 160
0 M 20 40 60 80 100
N

Davis & Harrison VP Ltd

△ *Flight-plan of the RAF raid on Mailly on 4/5 May 1944. The three-leg track took the 346 Lancasters north of Paris. Each red circle represents the place where a shot-down bomber crashed. Destroyed aircraft litter the ground north and south of the target.*
▷ *In Air Marshal Sir Arthur Harris's bombing interpretation room WAAF officers use stereoscopic equipment to give three-dimensional pictures of bomb damage to German targets. Great skill was needed to make correct interpretations of the results of the RAF's hits on the German military and industrial targets. Reports from saboteurs and agents near the targets would be added to the RAF's assessment of the raids.*

Popperfoto

normal approach height for a raid on Germany. Once the coast was crossed down went the bombers' noses and the Lancasters raced straight across N. France in order to arrive in the Mailly area at 5,000ft.

German air defenses responded and the first interceptions were made near Compiègne, but these resulted in bomber crews claiming the destruction of three night fighters with a fourth 'probably destroyed'. No bombers were lost in these early encounters—an unusual outcome to combats between fighters and bombers still fully loaded.

W/Cdr. Cheshire had arrived in the target area eight minutes before Zero Hour but had then flown on to a nearby airfield, pretending to be an Intruder ('hit and run' raider) so as not to alarm Mailly. On his return he found the camp bathed in the light of flares dropped by Lancasters of 83 and 97 Sqdns., every building being clearly visible. In a shallow dive down to 1,500ft Cheshire aimed two huge red markers —known as Red Spot Fires—at the first Aiming Point. These 'Red Spots' fell slightly NE of the target. Cheshire refused to allow bombing and called in another Mosquito to place fresh markers. Squadron Leader D. J. Shannon, one of the original 'Dambusters', dived to within 400ft of the ground to place his two Red Spot Fires in just the right place. Cheshire told W/Cdr. Deane, the Main Force Controller, that he was satisfied, Deane called in the first wave of Lancasters to bomb these markers.

Now, the first hint of trouble . . .

While Cheshire and his deputy carried out their careful marking of the target, the 140 (5 Group) Lancasters of the first wave had been orbiting at 5,000ft over a holding position, 15 miles north of Mailly, marked by yellow Target Indicators which cascaded in the air and then burned vividly on the ground. But now came the first hint of trouble.

S/Ldr. Shannon's markers had been placed at 0006 and immediately assessed as accurate—only four minutes behind schedule. Although W/Cdr. Deane immediately started calling the first wave of Lancasters in to bomb, only a few aircraft responded. Unfortunately the transmission on Deane's TR1196 VHF radio set could not be heard because a much stronger American news broadcast was drowning it. Deane tried the alternative method of communication, by morse through his wireless operator's T1154/R1155 set. Tragically, this also proved useless. Next morning, when the set was examined, it was found to be 30 kilocycles off frequency!

Some pilots had heard a garbled version of Deane's orders through the American broadcast and, when these bombed, a few more followed on their own initiative. These crews were the lucky ones. Their bomb-aimers were able to guide them over a well-marked and clearly visible target and from the unusually low bombing height found no difficulty in placing their five-ton HE loads on the German camp.

The best-placed observers were the Mosquito crews: 'When the bombing started it looked very effective. From our low-level position we could see very well; it was bright and men could be seen running from the barrack blocks to zig-zag trenches nearby. We flew around and dive-bombed the light flak positions which were hose-piping tracer up at the Main Force. When attacked, the guns stopped firing; whether this was due to our hits, fright or wisdom, I could not say'.

Cheshire, as marking force leader, was now in a cruel dilemma. The first markers were becoming obscured yet a few first wave Lancasters continued to bomb. Cheshire could see that an air battle would inevitably develop and was inclined to abandon further marking. He asked the Main Force Controller to bring the second wave straight in before too many aircraft were lost. W/Cdr. Deane attempted to pass on this order but again went unheard. Cheshire himself attempted to communicate directly with the Main Force, urging them to come in and bomb and even tried the extreme measure of ordering the raid to be abandoned and everyone to go home, but the Main Force never heard him.

The frustrated Cheshire now ordered in his two remaining Mosquito markers. Flight Lieutenants G. A. Fawke and R. S. D. Kearns, a New Zealander, dived to within 3,000ft of the ground and released their Red Spot Fires on the western end of the camp. Both pilots courageously flew across the target amid light flak while Lancasters continued to bomb, but their markers were soon lost to sight. One of the reserve Lancaster marker aircraft was now called to place its markers 'on the western edge of the fires with a slight undershoot'. Flying Officer H. W. J. Edwards of 97 Sqdn. flew in; his bomb-aimer, F/O J. Skingley, released the 10 Red Spots which almost filled the big Lancaster bomb bay and earned himself Cheshire's congratulations when the markers went down at the desired place.

The first Lancaster blew up

While all this was happening at Mailly there was serious trouble over the orbiting point 15 miles away. Many 5 Group aircraft had not heard the order to bomb and remained flying in wide circles above the ground marker. The 140 (1 Group) Lancasters of the second wave had arrived at the orbiting point and were also having to wait. The continued presence of over 200 heavy bombers 'marking time' above a bright yellow marker inevitably attracted German fighters. One Lancaster, detailed to back up the yellow marker, was chased right round its figure-of-eight marking pattern by a Junkers 88 but managed both to keep the markers going and shake off the German. But others were not so lucky and, with a sickening explosion in the sky, the first Lancaster blew up.

Most pilots were tuned in to one of the R/T channels and could, if they wished, themselves speak and be heard on the R/T set. Suddenly an angry voice came through, addressed to Cheshire: 'Pull your finger out!' It was not long before others joined in. The understandably frightened culprits would never be identified but this radio indiscipline unsettled other crews. It could only make the Controllers' work more difficult, and would probably be heard with glee by the Germans.

Suddenly, the Main Force pilots received their first clear orders: 'Don't bomb! Wait!' These came from S/Ldr. Sparks, the Deputy Controller. He had earlier only heard Deane's garbled voice through the American programme. Sparks had been in a quandary. If his chief had been shot down, it would have been Sparks' clear duty to take over but Deane was obviously present over Mailly and attempting to control the raid. Sparks had waited several minutes, but, with Deane still indistinct, decided to take charge using his aircraft's W/T transmitter. Later he even found a clear R/T channel on which to talk directly with the Main Force.

Spark's voice did not abate the radio panic. One tail gunner remembers: 'We circled and circled for what seemed an eternity without receiving any instructions. During this time German fighter activity became more intense. There was tracer everywhere and aircraft were going down in flames all around us, but still no instructions. One could

This Lancaster B1, serial No. ME703, carrying the letters UL (code letters of 576 Sqdn), got back from Mailly to make a crash-landing. It is likely both the rear turret and tail fin broke away during the forced landing and as the bomber slewed off the runway. It was luckier than the 42 Lancasters which failed to return from the shambles over Mailly on the night of 4/5 May 1944. Their crashes are plotted on the flight plan of the raid plotted on p.24

Bruce Robertson

sense the bombing force getting restless, like a herd ready to stampede and this was emphasised by the remarks made over the air, some of which should have turned the night sky blue, I heard one pilot's voice, "For Christ's sake shut up and give my gunners a chance". When I heard this remark I thought—"God help them if they are being attacked with this lot going on". But always the same stock phrase "Don't bomb! Wait!".'

Another, a pilot: 'I switched on for the Main Controller's commentary and was surprised to hear him ordering the Main Force to wait as the target had not yet been marked. The air was really blue with a succession of replies from the Main Force. I had never before heard R/T indiscipline and this was really the measure of the panic and fear that was abroad that night. This was quite enough for me—I had no intention of joining the crowd round those deathtrap markers, so we turned east towards the darker sky'. Still the protests came. 'We heard brief snatches of R/T, on one occasion what sounded like an English voice saying: "For Christ's sake! I am on fire!" This was replied to by a rough Australian voice saying: "If you are going to die, die like a man—quietly." A wing commander came up on the R/T, identified himself, and said: "This has got to stop. Cut your R/T and wait for instructions to bomb." But the frightened voices continued.'

More bombers went down. The Lancaster of Flight Sergeant George Gritty, No. 460 (Australian) Squadron, was caught by a single-engined fighter, easily identified in the bright moonlight as a Focke-Wulf 190. The German made three firing passes, then calmly stood off and watched the bomber burn. Three men baled out but then the flames reached the photo-flash and this, in turn, exploded the bombs. The Lancaster of F/Sgt. 'Lizzie' Lissette, a New Zealander of No. 207 Squadron, was also attacked by an FW 190. 'The tracer hit the port wing, blowing off the dinghy hatch. The dinghy then commenced to inflate, then shot back over the tailplane like a big hoopla ring. I could see down through the wing to the ground; the port under-carriage was partially down. A little later the rear gunner reported a fighter coming in port quarter down. We were hit again in the bomb bay and a small fire started.' A third attack soon finished off the Lancaster. The pilot remained at the controls to the end but again only three men out of seven baled out.

It was F/O Skingley's 10 Red Spot Fires, placed on the edge of the previous bombing area at Mailly, that ended this terrible wait. S/Ldr. Sparks now ordered: 'Go in and bomb. All aircraft go in and bomb. Bomb the Red Spot Fires.' The time was 0024, amazingly only five minutes behind schedule for the second wave bombing run.

One pilot, in his debriefing, reported that 'when the order to bomb was finally given the rush was like the starting gate at the Derby.' In these last few minutes the target became a veritable inferno. The huge, dull explosions of the 4,000lb 'blockbusters' and the shorter flashes of the 500lb HE gleamed through the dense clouds of dust and smoke billowing over the camp. Some flak was still firing. There were momentary but vivid photo-flashes dropped by every aircraft so that a bombing photograph could be taken. The Red Spot Fires were soon blown out or covered up and the bombing spread back across the open fields to the north of the camp. At 5,000ft the Lancasters were rocked by their own bomb explosions and by exploding ammunition dumps in the German camp. For crews used to bombing German cities from 20,000ft it was a novel and awesome experience.

Some aircraft that did not hear S/Ldr. Sparks's orders until as late as 0030 and the last aircraft did not bomb until 0044—19 minutes after the attack should have closed. The last pilot to fly across the target was the faithful Deputy Main Force Controller, Neville Sparks.

The delays at Mailly had given the Germans ample opportunity to direct their night fighters onto the bomber force. When the Lancasters turned for home, bright moon-light and the 'running commentary' put out by the German controllers enabled the *Nachtjagd* night fighter force to follow. One of these German fighters was a twin-engined Messerschmitt 110G-4/U1 of 4th Fighter Division piloted by *Hauptmann* Martin Drewes, whose airfield at Laon was only 65 miles from Mailly. Drewes' aircraft was one of the few fitted with the upward-firing *schräge Musik* ('Jazz Music') twin 30mm MK 108 cannon installation in the aft cockpit bulkhead. Such aircraft could abandon the traditional *von unten hinten* ('underneath, behind') method of attack, which at least gave the bomber's rear gunner a chance, and make their attack with cannon tilted at 15° fired by the pilot with the help of a Revi C/12D reflector sight in almost complete safety from the blind spot under-neath the bomber. Bomber Command had little knowledge of this weapon (first used in August 1943) and crews had not been warned of it. Drewes' radar operator, *Unteroffizier* Erich Handke, describes their experiences.

'We saw the target burning and this enabled us to get into the bomber stream. I guided my pilot with the *SN-2* (a radar set) onto a bomber and, at 600 metres, we could see it by

A trolley load of 500lb bombs, already fuzed, about to go into the Lancaster's capacious bomb-bay.

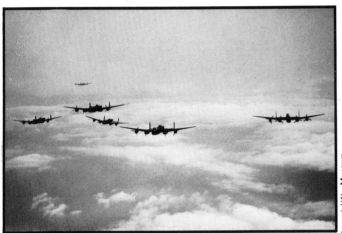

For bombers there is protection in numbers. With some cloud cover, these Lancasters are on way to target.

A marker flare lights up the target area early in the Mailly raid, before the buildings were destroyed.

eye. The weather was wonderful, almost full moon. We sat under the Lancaster which was only at 2,400 metres height. We shot from underneath into the wing which burned at once. Almost immediately the bomber went down in flames. I had already found another target; it was flying away to the west at 2,000 metres—another Lancaster. We got 500 metres underneath it and then climbed to within about 70 metres. We fired this time into the fuselage because we could now be sure there were no bombs there. There was a huge fire and it soon crashed.'

'We saw another aircraft straight ahead but lower, and we were soon underneath. We climbed a little then fired vertically with our *schräge Musik*. It burned and soon went down. The next one was spotted by Petz (the rear gunner) and once more we got into an attacking position but this time the Lancaster was climbing and we could not fire for some time until it settled down at 3,000 metres. After a long burst of fire into the fuselage the entire tail unit broke off and the remainder burst into bright flames and crashed.'

Within minutes, Drewes and his crew found themselves flying within sight of four more Lancasters but it took Drewes 20 minutes to get into a firing position underneath what Handke describes as 'the most peaceful one'. This 'kill' almost fell on top of the Me 110 and Drewes had to dive steeply to avoid his flaming victim. The five Lancasters Drewes and his crew had downed within 40 minutes brought their total score to 45 victories.

'I had at most two minutes . . .'

S/Ldr. Sparks was to pay for staying so long over Mailly: 'As we left the target my rear gunner, Warrant Officer 'Tiger' Teague, reported four fighters on our tail. I immediately started a corkscrew intending to lose height rapidly from 3,000ft to return as near ground level as possible and I took a straight line from Mailly towards England. During our second steep bank to the left I saw another fighter directly beneath us, perhaps 1,000ft below. I pressed on with the corkscrew but this chap somehow put perhaps a dozen cannon shells into my starboard wing fuel tanks. We had no nitrogen suppression and in a short time the top skin of the wing had burnt through with a mass of flame. I had seen so many Lancasters with burning wings that I knew my aircraft had at most two minutes before the main spar failed with a consequent uncontrollable spin.

'I gave the order to bale out in my No. 2 method which was unofficial but known and practised by my crew. This method was that the crew were to get up and get out without delay and any intercom. This they did and I was sitting there keeping an eye on the burning wing and calling up all crew positions to check that no one was left on board. None was, and all lived. As I was calling the last position, the wing folded up and I immediately made a turning dive through the front hatch.'

The French Resistance found Sparks and told him that his rear gunner had shot down one of the German fighters. Sparks was back with his squadron at Coningsby seven weeks later.

Another return route combat was observed by a Lancaster pilot: 'I have a clear memory of the full bright moon without a cloud in the sky and of watching an FW 190 shooting down a Lanc from the stern. The fighter then carried on under the Lanc, drew ahead of a second bomber, then pulled up into a loop and half-rolled on the top. He then attacked the second Lanc head on and shot him down also. German or not, it was first-class flying and I could not but admire his technique. Needless to say I opened all four throttles and got the hell out of the place'.

Occasionally, bomber crews were able to hit back. One crew, on their first operation, chased a German fighter down to ground level and shot it down; the pilot and tail gunner, both Australians, won the Distinguished Flying Cross and Distinguished Flying Medal respectively. Another Lancaster crew shot down a fighter but their own aircraft was damaged so badly that all engines failed just before reaching the diversion airfield at Tangmere, Sussex. The New Zealand pilot made a successful glide-landing. The Operational Record Book of 97 Sqdn. shows that its crews used their initiative: 'Many of our aircraft flew at heights between fifty and 200ft above the ground often flying down German-occupied aerodromes, strafing searchlights and flak towers.'

The fortunes of war had not been kind to the bomber crews, but the Germans did not follow them over the Channel, no damaged aircraft crashed into the sea, and clear weather at their Lincolnshire airfields enabled survivors to land safely.

Out of 346 Lancasters that took off to bomb Mailly-le-Camp, 42 failed to return and two more were so badly damaged that they had to be written off. No. 5 Group, which supplied nearly all the marker aircraft and the entire first wave, lost 14 of its 173 Lancasters. No. 1 Group, dispatching another 173 Lancasters, suffered exactly twice 5 Group's losses. Its aircraft had been subject to the greatest delay at Mailly and 28 were lost—a casualty rate of 16 per cent. The hardest hit squadron of the 24 bombing was the Australian 460 Sqdn. from Binbrook—it had lost five crews; Nos 12, 50 and 101 Sqdns each lost four crews. One Intruder Mosquito and one Radio-Counter-Measures Halifax were also shot down.

Success for the 'Wild Boar'

The Germans claimed to have destroyed 57 four-engined bombers against actual losses of 44 over Mailly and three more on another raid. The Me 110 units of 4th Fighter Division (100 serviceable fighters on 31 May) stationed at Florennes, Coulommiers, Saint-Dizier and Laon achieved most of this success but single-engined FW 190 *Wilde Sau* ('Wild Boar') fighters, working without radar but by searchlight, moonlight and the bombers 'marker flares', scored at least four 'kills'. In return, the Mailly raiders claimed eight German fighters destroyed and two 'probables'.

Approximately 1,500 tons of bombs were dropped on Mailly—what had been achieved? Reconnaissance photographs taken two days later showed a great mass of bomb craters especially in the barrack blocks. No fewer than 114 barrack buildings, 47 transport sheds and workshops, and some ammunition stores had been hit.

According to *Bundesarchiv* records the camp housed a *Panzer* regiment HQ, three *Panzer* battalions (belonging to regiments on the Eastern Front) and elements of two more as well as the permanent training school staff. Casualties were 218 men listed as killed or missing and 156 wounded. More permanent staff were killed than men from visiting units and a high proportion of the dead were highly trained NCOs. The 102 vehicles destroyed included 37 tanks. Damage to the buildings was German assessed as '80 per cent destroyed, 20 per cent worth repairing.'

Bomber Command would have been disappointed to learn that only 374 Germans had been disabled when its own aircrew losses were around 300. The slight delay in the initial marking, and the slow development of the attack due

to W/Cdr. Deane's difficulties, had given the Germans the opportunity to take shelter.

The *Bundesarchiv* report contains an interesting reference to a Sergeant Jack Worsfold, rear gunner in a 101 Sqdn. Lancaster, who had an almost miraculous escape when his aircraft was hit over Mailly. The rear turret broke away and fell with Worsford trapped inside, but its fall was broken by some electricity cables, and he was able to walk away dazed but unhurt. The Germans thought that Worsfold was an agent dropped at Mailly to report on the raid. It was some time before they accepted him as an ordinary airman.

Many crews who had returned to England were naturally bitter at the costly delays. In 1 Group there was much criticism of 5 Group in general and of Cheshire in particular; he was thought to have been unnecessarily careful about the marking. This was unfair. The complicated plan and the communications failures were the main causes of the delay.

The least glorious aspect of the raid had been the radio indiscipline of the crews held back at the orbiting point. So far as is known, this never occurred on any other bombing operation. But some of these men had flown right through the past winter with its hard-fought series of raids on distant targets. Many had survived the Nuremberg raid five weeks earlier (30/31 March) when nearly 100 crews were lost. On this night over Mailly they had been psychologically geared up to fly on a short-range, 'easy target'. It only counted as one third of an operation—a rule which was immediately altered—yet they had found themselves waiting apparently without orders, flying round a beacon while German fighters blew Lancasters to pieces around them.

But despite delay, danger and radio panic, there is no evidence that any crew failed to carry out its duty. There was no wild or scattered bombing. Enquiries at Mailly-le-Camp showed that not one civilian was killed by bombs although some were killed by crashing bombers. The men who flew to Mailly-le-Camp may have shown fear. They did not show cowardice.

Martin Middlebrook

1 *The* Panzer *training camp at Mailly before the raid of 4/5 May. Zig-zag slit trenches had been dug in the grounds of the former French Army establishment.*
2 *A Mk 1 Lancaster in night operations coloring.*
3 *The same area as Pic 1 after the RAF's attack. Practically every building is destroyed or damaged. Near-misses on slit-trenches would have caused casualties from blast and concussion. The workshop area (top left) has been particularly badly hit.*
4 *A wider view of the area of Mailly. The accuracy of the RAF's bomb-aimers and their Mk XIV sights is clearly demonstrated. Nearby fields have no more than a sprinkling of bomb craters.*

Peter Sarson/Tony Bryan

NACHTJAGD

Germany's elite fighter force faces the Allies' big bombers

Addressing his officers in August 1940, Colonel Josef Kammhuber remarked: 'Yes, gentlemen, I hear only about difficulties in your descriptions. But don't keep on about the old problem of trying to catch a fly in a darkened room.'

'Like trying to catch a fly in a darkened room' is the German equivalent of the English saying 'Like trying to find a needle in a haystack'—trying to do what is barely, if at all, possible. That was certainly how things looked to the *Luftwaffe* in the summer of 1940. Officers and men had hastily been gathered together to form a night fighter force to combat the nocturnal British raids on Germany. From this shaky foundation the organization which Kammhuber built up was to become one of the most efficient in the *Luftwaffe*, inflicting heavy losses on RAF Bomber Command. At the peak of its effectiveness, on the night of 30/31 March 1944, the force managed to destroy about 80 of the 107 heavy bombers the RAF lost that night. But, from then until the end of the war the German night fighter force came under ever-increasing pressure. Its effectiveness gradually slumped. But the Allies could never ignore it. To the very end it proved capable of springing unpleasant surprises. Such was the *Nachtjagd*.

From the beginning of World War II until May 1940, the night air defense of German industrial areas had been entrusted to the *Flak* (AA) arm of the *Luftwaffe*. At that time the only night fighters available were a few single-engined planes—mostly Me 109s—flown by pilots who had specialized in the role. Because of the small number of night fighters, the lack of any effective ground control, and above all the few RAF bombers operating over Germany (most of them leaflet raiders), the Germans achieved hardly any 'kills' during this period.

The great change came on 14 May 1940 when, following the destructive German bombing attack on Rotterdam,

△ A Luftwaffe *aristocrat*, Major Prinz *Heinrich zu Sayn Wittgenstein. Killed over Magdeburg on 21 January 1944. He had 83 victories as a night-fighter pilot. On the night he was killed in action, shot down by a Mosquito, he had attacked and downed four RAF heavy bombers.*
▷ *An* Oberleutnant *in* Fleugerbluse *and late-pattern one-piece flying suit. He wears night-fighter insignia.*

Malcolm McGregor

▷ An Me 110-G4/R1, with early 1943 Lichtenstein radar.

◁ The 416mph He 219A-5/R1 carrying both Lichtenstein *SN-2 (large)* radar and the C1 for close-range seeking. This night-fighter was armed with two 30mm MK 108 cannon in the ventral position, twin wing-root cannon and the unconventional Schrage Musik *('Jazz Music')* upwards-firing 30mm MK 108 cannon.

Bundesarchiv

Prime Minister Winston Churchill ordered RAF Bomber Command to open its offensive against industrial targets in Germany. During the three weeks that followed RAF bombers flew about 1,700 night sorties over Germany and lost only 39 aircraft—most of them in accidents. Clearly the *Flak* defenses, alone, could not deter such assaults.

The man charged with this task was Colonel Kammhuber. A stocky Bavarian, he was nearly 44 when he took up his appointment in July 1940. During World War I he had fought as an infantryman. He remained in the army after the war. In 1933 he transferred to the secret *Luftwaffe* and at the time of the Flanders campaign in May 1940 commanded a bomber *geschwader.* He was shot down by French fighters and captured, but his captivity was short-lived and he was freed when the French signed the armistice. Soon after his return to Germany he received his orders to expand and improve the night fighter organization. The early British attacks on targets in the Ruhr and western Germany had not been particularly damaging.

By the end of July 1940 Kammhuber's force was much bigger than it had been when he took office, but it was still very small. In addition to the single-engined Me109s available at the beginning, there were now two *Staffeln* of Me110s and a few of the new Ju88 fighters—about 35 planes in all. The two latter types were twin-engined aircraft, with the greater endurance and extra crew member which made them more suitable for night operations. Backing this force on the ground was one regiment of searchlights and a few *Freya* early-warning radar sets. Soon after his appointment Kammhuber was promoted to *Generalmajor.* He set up his headquarters in a beautiful seventeenth century castle at Zeist near Utrecht in Holland.

Night fighting was still in its infancy. Generally the fighters took off after receiving radar warning of the approach of the raiders, and orbited radio beacons until searchlights illuminated the bomber. Once they had spotted their targets, the fighter pilots closed in for the kill. This system achieved some successes, and was known as 'illuminated night fighting' (*Helle Nachtjagd*). It did, however, have serious faults. Since the searchlights were almost always positioned near towns, these tactics rarely achieved anything outside the target areas. Moreover, as they orbited over these defended areas the night fighters themselves were often illuminated and engaged by German AA gunners. To overcome these problems Kammhuber shifted his night fighter engagement area so as to be clear of the German cities—therefore outside the gun-defended areas. The searchlight batteries were moved out to positions along a line running from Schleswig-Holstein in northern Germany to Liege in Belgium—astride the route used by RAF bombers attacking Germany.

Up to this time there had been a great deal of improvisation. But Kummhuber was busy laying a firmer foundation for his force. From the start he had seen that if they were really to 'catch the fly in the darkened room', his men would need the best equipment that German technology could provide. Any system dependent on searchlights was a slave to the weather. Fifty per cent cloud cover could make it inoperative. What was needed was a night interception technique which did not rely on searchlights, but this in its turn called for a radar set with which a ground controller could guide a night fighter to its target. The *Freya* radar already in service was really not up to the job. Its definition was too poor, so that the blips of the night fighter and the bomber merged on the screen long before the fighter pilot could make visual contact with his target. A new precision gunnery control radar, the *Wuerzburg* produced by the Telefunken company, promised to be much better for this purpose. Kammhuber had orders placed for a large number of these for his force.

During 1941 the production of the new *Wuerzburg* radar got into its stride and these sets were delivered to the ground stations set up at 20-mile distances along Kammhuber's air defense line. As well as a *Freya* for early warning, each station received two of the new precision radars, one to track the German night fighter and the other to track the enemy bomber. With the relative positions of both aircraft displayed on the screen in front of him, the ground controller passed instructions to the night fighter pilot to bring him to a position within visual range behind the bomber. These new tactics bore the code-name *Himmelbett* ('four-poster bed').

Apart from the defensive work of Kammhuber's force there was one unit engaged on offensive intruder operations over Britain. This was the First *Gruppe* of *Nachtjagd-geschwader 2* with some 30 Ju88s and Do17s. These aircraft were ordered up when RAF bombers were engaged in raids, and patrolled over the latters' bases trying to catch them when they returned. Bombers on their final approach for landing had little reserve speed for evasion and were virtually 'sitting ducks'—a fact known all too well to their crews.

Few bombers were actually shot down by the German intruders—but the effect on British morale was considerable.

The already-tired bomber crews were forced to land on dimly-lit airfields, and there were several cases of aircraft being damaged or written-off in heavy landings. There could be no thought of 'going round again', no matter how bad the approach, if there were intruders about. But, in the autumn of 1941 the sortage of night fighter units to operate with the expanding number of *Himmelbett* ground stations, coupled with the general over-extension of the *Luftwaffe* as the Russian campaign imposed its demands, led to a cessation of these operations. *I/NJG 2* assumed the defensive role. After this, no German unit was regularly and exclusively engaged in intruder operations over the British airfields.

By the second half of 1941 the *Nachtjagd* had grown into a powerful force with some 250 twin-engined fighters, Me110s, Ju88s and Do17s. This impressive force was backed by an increasingly effective ground control and reporting organization.

Menace of the 'inverted sickle'

Between the summer of 1941 and the summer of 1942 the line of *Himmelbett* stations stretched until it ran from the northern tip of Denmark to the Swiss frontier. This defensive barrier was shaped like an inverted sickle—its 'handle' running through Denmark from north to south and its 'blade' curving through northern Germany, Holland, Belgium and eastern France. In the late spring of 1942 RAF Bomber Command began concentrating its aircraft in tight 'streams', which saturated the *Himmelbett* defenses along the route. Kammhuber responded by building additional ground stations both in front and behind his line. This increased its width, thus increasing the number of bombers tied up in any one attack.

Also during 1942 two new radar sets began to enter service in quantity, to improve the efficiency of the *Nachtjagd*. The first was the *Wuerzburg Reise* ('Giant') which had a longer range and began to replace the early Wuerzburg sets at the ground *Himmelbett* stations. Secondly, the lightweight *Lichtenstein* airborne radar was fitted into the night fighters themselves.

By the end of 1942 the German night fighter force totalled 389 aircraft. The great majority of these were Me110s with a few Ju88s and a sprinkling of Do217s. During that year the RAF lost 1,291 bombers by all causes during attacks on Germany and occupied Europe. It is estimated that two-thirds of these fell to night fighters.

It is of interest to examine the *Himmelbett* system, as it operated during the early months of 1943. On the night of 21/22 June RAF Bomber Command sent a force of 705 aircraft to attack the town of Krefeld on the western edge of the Ruhr industrial area. At 0054 on the 22nd *Leutnant* Heinz-Wolfgang Schnaufer lifted his Me110G off the ground at St Trond in Belgium and climbed into the darkness to his patrol areas overhead *Himmelbett* station *Meise* (Tomtit)—15 miles NE of Brussels.

At *Meise* the men of the 13th Company of the 211th *Luftwaffe* Signals Regiment used their *Freya* radar to search for 'trade' coming into their area from the west. Just after 0120 they spotted an aircraft which, if it continued on its heading, would come plum into their engagement range. Since German aircraft were forbidden entry into the *Himmelbett* belt without permission, there was little doubt that the contact was hostile. One of the *Wuerzburg Reise* precision radars was already tracking Schnaufer's aircraft, the other swung round and began searching in the area

indicated by the *Freya*. Even before it had made contact *Leutnant* Kuehnel, the fighter control officer at *Meise*, ordered Schnaufer on to a westerly heading towards the incoming aircraft. At 0126 the crew of the second *Wuerzburg Reise* made contact with the target. With precise information on the whereabouts of both the pursuer and the pursued, Kuehnel radioed Schnaufer a steady stream of instructions as the two aircraft converged almost head-on. Just before the two planes crossed, the night fighter was ordered to turn through 180°. Schnaufer pulled his aircraft round, and slid neatly in behind the target. The enemy crew still suspected nothing. In the rear of the Messerschmitt *Leutnant* Baro huddled over the flickering screens of the *Lichtenstein* radar. Suddenly he saw what he was looking for— a small hump of light rising up from the blue base line, a target at 2,734 yards (2,500m or about 1½ miles). Baro broadcast a quick *Pauke!* call, and Kuehnel ceased his commentary. (*Pauke*—literally 'beat the kettle-drum'—meant 'I have the enemy in contact and am about to engage'. It was the equivalent of the RAF's 'Tally Ho!').

Now it was Baro's turn to guide Schnaufer to his target, still beyond visual range in the black sky ahead. Gradually the Messerschmitt closed in until at 0130, in the words of the report Schnaufer wrote afterwards: 'I recognised, 500 metres above and to the right, a Short Stirling and succeeded in getting in an attack on the violently evading enemy aircraft. It caught fire in the fuselage and the wings and continued on, burning, Then it went into a vertical dive and crashed 3 kilometres to the north-east of Aerschot.'

At dawn *Leutnant* Kuehnel set out from the *Himmelbett* station to the scene of the crash, to confirm the 'kill'. Afterwards he reported:

Schnaufer's 13th victory

'At 6am on 22.6.43 I was at the scene of the crash of the Short Stirling shot down by Lt Schnaufer at 0133½ hours on 22.6.43. The wreckage was 3 kilometres to the north-east of Aerschot, map reference NK 31b. There was a crew of 7, all of whom were lying dead in the wreckage. The Short Stirling was completely wrecked in the crash and the subsequent fire; the rudder and the rear gun turret were some 1,500 metres from the remainder of the wreckage.' It had been Schnaufer's 13th victory. RAF losses that night totalled 42 aircraft.

June 1943 was outstandingly successful for the German night fighter and *Flak* defense. During that month they caused the destruction of more than 275 of the night raiders—about three-quarters of them to the fighters. But retribution was coming.

On 25 July the RAF introduced its answer to the uncomfortably efficient German night defenses—'Window'. 'Window' was the code name given to strips of metal foil. Each one of these was cut to 30cm by 1.5cm, which was about one half the wavelength of the German precision radars. In their haste to bring their sets into service, the Germans made the mistake of running both the giant and the small *Wuerzburg* sets—and the *Lichtenstein* in the night fighters—on almost exactly the same radio frequency. They were soon to learn the error of their ways, for the metal strips of the same length effectively jammed all of the most important German sets. Bundles dropped at a rate of one a minute from each aircraft in the attacking force broke up to form clouds of radar-reflective strips. The 'clouds' merged to form an electronic 'smokescreen' which effectively

▷ A Wellington's rear-turret being armed with .303 continuous belt ammo by three careful Sgt. Air Gunners. Their lives may depend on ammunition belts not failing under attack.
▽▷ Nose of the Do 217J-2 clad in the Lichtenstein aerial array, and showing also the formidable group of four drum-fed 20mm Oerlikon MG FF cannon.
▽ On the front of the dais during a 1941 march-past are Generalmajor Josef Kammhuber who planned the Himmelbett system of radar fighter control, and Helmut Lent, Paul Gilder and Ludwig Bekker, three aces.

concealed the raiders from the defenders. Radar-controlled gun or fighter engagements became impossible.

The new countermeasure was used for the first time in action by a force of 791 bombers attacking Hamburg. It reduced the German night fighter and *Flak* defenses to chaos. Only 12 aircraft—1.5 per cent of the force, were lost during the action. Had the raid cost the 6 per cent loss usual for an attack on such a heavily defended target, RAF Bomber Command would have lost about 50 planes. During three equally successful follow-up attacks during the eight nights that followed, 50,000 people were killed and large sections of Hamburg were razed to the ground.

Following the Hamburg disaster, the German night fighter tactics underwent a sweeping reorganization. The *Himmelbett* system of close-controlled interceptions was now unworkable and was replaced by two new tactical methods —'Wild Boar' and 'Tame Boar'. The 'Wild Boar' tactics called for the operation of fighters over the target itself. where the massed searchlights and the bombers' own marker flares lit up the sky for miles around and silhouetted the raiders. Once illuminated, they could be attacked by fighters not using radar. This was important. It meant that jamming by 'Window' could have no effect. The main difference between 'Wild Boar' and the initial 'illuminated night fighting' tactics was one of scale. Now there were

more bombers over the targets, a great deal more illumination, and far more fighters to engage the raiders. Major Hajo Herrmann, the leading proponent of the 'Wild Boar' tactics, received orders to form a full *Geschwader*—about 90 aircraft—to exploit the new tactics. Once 'Wild Boar' fighters were in action over a target, *Flak* units on the ground below had orders to engage bombers only up to a designated altitude—usually 19,500ft.

The radar-equipped twin-engined night fighters could also join in the 'Wild Boar' battles at the target. But to use their potential to the full they employed their own 'Tame Boar' tactics. Under this system the fighter divisional HQ on the ground broadcast a running commentary on the postion of the bomber stream, together with orders to the fighters to make for radio beacons in the path of the raiders. The night fighter crews were to use their radar to get into the points where the 'Window' concentrations were densest, and on arrival search for their quarry visually.

With these sweeping tactical changes, the night fighter force received a new commander—*Generalmajor* Josef Schmidt. *Generalmajor* Kammhuber had built up the *Nachtjagd* almost from scratch. But in so doing he had frequently come into bitter disagreement with Goering. As long as Kammhuber's methods worked, and took a high toll of the raiders, however, it was not easy for the *Reichsmarschall* to

Bundesarchiv

oust him. But, with the neutralisation of *Himmelbett,* Goering lost little time in shunting its architect off to a backwater post in Norway. Schmidt had a more pliable attitude than his predecessor. Like Kammhuber, Schmidt had come originally from the army and had transferred to the secret *Luftwaffe* in 1933. But after that Schmidt had confined his career to that of a staff officer—his most noteworthy post being that of head of the *Luftwaffe* intelligence department from 1938 to 1942. He had never been in charge of a flying unit before he took command of the *Nachtjagd.*

During the latter part of 1943 three new airborne electronic devices entered service—*SN-2 Naxos* and *Flensburg.* The *SN-2* was a completely new radar set for night fighters, to replace the earlier *Lichtenstein.* It worked on radio frequencies outside those jammed by the types of 'Window' then used by the RAF. *Naxos* and *Flensburg* were both radar homing devices. The former worked on emissions from the navigational radar fitted to British bombers and the latter on the emissions from their tail-warning radar.

In early 1944, a typical 'Tame Boar' operation would begin with German night fighter crews relaxing but in readiness in dimly lit huts close to their aircraft dispersals. They were kept informed of the progress of the enemy bombers by broadcast announcements. There was usually plenty of warning of the approach of the raiders—especially for units based in central Germany—and the crewing-up and starting of the aircraft were generally accomplished without undue haste. As the night fighters taxied out to the take-off point their radio operators tuned in to the *Reichsjagerwelle,* the fighter broadcast frequency, for up-to-date information on the position, probable strength, heading and believed destination of the raiders, as well as the radio beacons they were to make for after take-off. As soon as they were airborne, the night fighters would climb to the bombers' usual 20,000ft. altitude.

As the bomber stream moved deeper into German-occupied territory its intentions became clearer to the German ground controllers, who broadcast orders to the night fighters to converge on beacons in the raiders' path. When the bombers were close enough, the night fighters were ordered to leave their beacon at a set heading and seek out the enemy on their own. Often, the first indication

of the presence of the raiders was that the night fighter's radio operator picked up their emissions on his *Naxos* or *Flensburg* receivers. On other occasions he would see them first on his *SN-2* radar. Sometimes, however, the first indication of enemy aircraft was the judder felt by the night fighter as it passed through the tubulent wake left by the stream of heavy bombers.

Once they had located the bomber stream, the *Nachtjagd* crews had strict orders not to attack before they had passed to ground control the heading and position of the bombers. This information was relayed to other night fighters.

Having gained visual contact with a bomber, a night fighter pilot would try to approach it from slightly below. In that way he remained difficult to see against the dark background of the earth, while the bomber was silhouetted against the sky. The ideal attack position was considered to be underneath and slightly to the rear of a bomber. Attacks were made with upwards-firing cannon (code-named *Schraege Musik*). Alternatively, the German pilot would pull up the nose of his aircraft and rake the bomber with his forward-firing cannon. The most popular aiming point was the wing on either side of one of the engines. These contained the inflammable fuel tanks. Since the night fighters attacked from short ranges—often within 75 yards— it was not thought wise to aim at the bomber's fuselage and risk detonating the bomb load and destroying the fighter in the resulting explosion.

At the beginning of 1944, the top-scoring German night fighter pilot was *Major* Prinz Heinrich zu Sayn Wittgenstein, whose victory total had reached 79 by the third week in the new year. The combat report written by Wittgenstein's radar operator, *Feldwebel* Ostheimer, after the action on 21 January 1944 clearly describes the sort of hard-fought battles that were taking place in the night skies over Germany at this time:

'At 2200 I picked up the first contact on my *SN-2* search equipment. I passed the pilot directions and a little later the target was sighted: it was a Lancaster. We moved into position and opened fire, and the aircraft immediately caught fire in the left wing. It went down at a steep angle and started to spin. Between 2200 and 2205 the bomber crashed and went off with a violent explosion; I watched the crash.

MESSERSCHMITT 110 G-4b/R3

Peter Sarson/Tony Bryan

Mansell Collection

Bundesarchiv

◁△ *Backbone of the German night-fighter force from 1940 until 1941, the Me 110 went through the Bf 110B-1 to the Bf 110H-4.* △ *An Me 110G-4b/R3 complete with* Lichtenstein SN-2 *long-range radar and* FUG 212 C-1 *200-yard range radar. The aircraft is fitted with two 66 Imp. gall. drop tanks below the outboard wing-panels.* ▷ *Insignia of the German night-intruder force— 'Englandblitz'. Lightning strikes at a feeble map of England.* ▷▷ Luftwaffe *armorers working on the upper nose panel of an Me 110 night-fighter. Note the large 'Englandblitz' emblem.*

'Again we searched. At times I could see as many as six aircraft on my radar. After some further directions the next target was sighted—again a Lancaster. Following the first burst from us there was a small fire, and the machine dropped back on its left wing and went down in a vertical dive. Shortly afterwards I saw it crash. It was some time between 2210 and 2215. When it crashed there were heavy detonations, most probably it was the bomb load.

'After a short interval we again sighted a Lancaster. There was a long burst of fire and the bomber ignited and went down. I saw it crash some time between 2225 and 2230; the exact time is not known.

'Immediately afterwards we saw yet another four-motored bomber—we were in the middle of the so-called 'bomber stream'. After one firing pass this bomber went down in flames; at about 2240 I saw the crash.

'Yet again I had a target on my search equipment. After a few directions we again sighted a Lancaster and after one attack it caught fire in the fuselage. The fire then died down,

and we moved into position for a new attack. We were again in position and *Major* Wittgenstein was ready to shoot when, in our own machine, there were terrible explosions and sparks. It immediately caught fire in the left wing and began to go down. As I heard this the canopy above my head flew away and I heard on the intercom a shout of *"Raus!"* ("Get out!"). I tore off my oxygen mask and helmet, and was then thrown out of the machine. After a short time I opened my parachute, and landed east of the Hohengoehrener Dam, near Schoenhausen.'

The following day Wittgenstein's body was found in the wreckage of his Ju88. Two of the returning bombers afterwards reported having shot down Ju88s in the target area. It would seem that one of those was that flown by the Prince.

During the night's attacks, on Berlin and Magdeburg, RAF Bomber Command lost a total of 56 aircraft. Of these, 13 were seen to go down to *Flak*. The 43 others probably fell to night fighters. After the action German night fighter

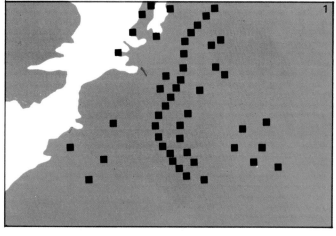

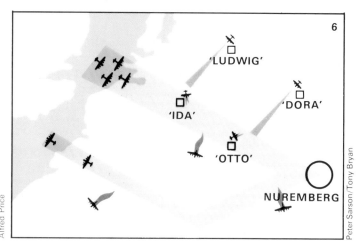

Alfred Price

Peter Sarson/Tony Bryan

1 *Himmelbett stations in Occupied Europe.*
2 *Fighter orbits and waits as 'Freya' locks on bomber.*
3 *'Wurzberg' radar (green) fixes bomber and fighter.*
4 *Fighter's own 'Lichtenstein' radar homes on bomber.*
5 *The Giant Wurzberg radar aerial, range 40 miles.*
6 *Radio and visual beacons Ludwig, Ida, Dora, Otto.*

crews were allowed 37 confirmed 'kills' and four 'probables'. Bearing in mind the very close agreement between the British and the German figures, there is little reason to doubt the accuracy of Ostheimer's claim for his dead pilot.

As the new year progressed, the German defenses were able to inflict heavy blows. On 28 January 43 bombers were shot down out of 683 attacking Berlin. The following month the *Nachtjagd* was even more successful. On 15 February the RAF lost 42 bombers out of 891 attacking Berlin, and four days later 78 out of 823 over Leipzig. In March, 72 out of 811 despatched were lost during the attack on Berlin on the 24th.

The climax of this phase of the bombing offensive came on the night of 30/31 March. A force of 781 Lancasters and

Halifaxes set out to attack Nuremburg. It was a bright moonlight night and the temperature was so low that the bombers streamed behind them dense white condensation trails—a fairly rare phenomenon at the 20,000ft altitudes at which they operated. That night the German fighter control organisation worked to perfection and 21 *Gruppen* of 'Tame Boar' night fighters—about 200 aircraft—took off to engage the raiders. The result was a long running-battle

JUNKERS 88G-1

Peter Sarson/Tony Bryan

△ The Ju 88G-1, carrying Lichtenstein SN-2 radar aerials instead of the C-1 assembly.
▷ This Ju 88G-1 belonging to Nachtjagd 2 landed at Woodbridge, Essex. Its pilot had flown a reciprocal course instead of his correct compass course. This took him in the opposite direction from his home field. The radar equipment was of great interest to the RAF.

Alfred Price

which ended in disaster for the British force. A total of 107 heavy bombers were destroyed—another 24 suffering damage. About 50 'Wild Boar' single-engined fighters were scrambled, but these failed to make contact.

At this, the high-water mark of its existence, *Nachtjagd* comprised 565 twin-engined fighters—Ju88s, Me110s, He219s and Do217s. In addition, the 'Wild Boar' units operated about 100 single-engined Me109s and FW190s.

Following the Nuremburg operation the RAF heavy bombers temporarily stopped their attacks on Germany, and engaged in 'softening-up' operations in preparation for the invasion of France. Back in the Reich the *Nachtjagd* stood ready, confident in its ability to strike telling blows whenever Bomber Command resumed its attacks on Germany. But the defenders were past their peak. One reason for the German successes at the beginning of 1944 had been the veil of secrecy which had concealed the night fighters' electronic devices—SN-2, *Naxos* and *Flensburg*—from British Intelligence. On 13 July 1944 most of this covering was torn away when a Ju88 carrying SN-2 and *Flensburg* inadvertently landed at the RAF airfield, Woodbridge in Essex. RAF experts eagerly examined the windfall and their new-found knowledge was quickly applied. Within 10 days Bomber Command aircraft were using a new type of 'Window' which jammed the frequency used by SN-2. The strips of foil had as great an effect on this radar as they had had on *Lichtenstein* almost exactly a year earlier. Shortly afterwards the RAF also became aware of the existence of *Naxos.*

The period from the summer of 1944 until the end of the war was, for the German night fighter force, one of unremitting decline. The increasing weight and effectiveness of the RAF radar jamming, the fuel shortage and the end of all

flying training in the *Luftwaffe* which followed it, the increasing degree of Allied air superiority over Germany both by day and by night and, finally, the inexorable advance of the Allied ground forces, all combined to decrease the effectiveness of the force.

To the very end, however, the *Nachtjagd* could still spring unpleasant surprises. Its final fling came on 3 March 1945, following a two-pronged attack by 456 RAF bombers on targets at Kamen and Ladbergen. As the bombers withdrew and made for their bases in eastern England, more than 100 German night fighters scrambled into the air and headed westwards in hot pursuit. The *Luftwaffe* was launching its long-planned operation *Gisella*, the first large-scale intruder operation against the bomber airfields since the late summer of 1941. Two waves of aircraft, comprising mainly Ju88s but with a few He219s, swept over the North Sea and made for targets in Norfolk, Suffolk, Lincolnshire and Yorkshire. A total of 27 airfields came under attack from cannon, MG fire and small bombs. As well as the bombers returning from Germany, the intruders were able to catch many aircraft engaged in training flights. In all, 48 RAF aircraft came under attack—of which 22 were shot down and a further eight suffered damage. The British defenses claimed to have shot down six of the attackers. For the Germans *Gisella* had been a successful operation, but it was never to be repeated on such a large scale. On the night of 17 March, a force of 18 Ju88s took off from Holland for a similar attack on the RAF bases. But on this occasion no bomber operations were in progress and the intruders were able to destroy only one British plane on a training flight. So it was that the *Nachtjagd,* in its own death throes, carried out the final offensive action against the British Isles during World War II.   **Alfred Price**

NUREMBERG

A night when the German Nachtjagd 'came good'. As dawn broke, the wreckage of 94 RAF heavy bombers blazed on the ground

C. Bowyer/I.W.M.

Apart from being one of the cradles of Nazism and scene of some of that creed's most spectacular and hysterical rallies, the Bavarian city of Nuremberg was an important center for war production. Inside its boundaries were the huge *Machinenfabrik Augsburg-Nürnberg* producing diesel engines for tanks and U-boats, the Siemens factory making electrical equipment for the German navy, the Zundapp motor works turning out vehicles for the Army, and in addition, the city was an important rail center. With a population of about 330,000 people, Nuremberg could be compared, in terms of size and importance within the wartime economy, with Coventry in Warwickshire, England.

On the morning of Thursday 30 March, 1944, aircrews at RAF Bomber Command airfields along the eastern side of England were given their next target, Code-named Grayling. All German targets had been given the names of fish by Air Marshal Sir Robert Saundby, an enthusiastic angler, the Deputy Commander-in-Chief, Bomber Command.

The battle orders had come by clattering teleprinter from Air Chief Marshal Sir Arthur T. ('Bomber') Harris's underground Bomber Command HQ, situated in the hills above High Wycombe in Buckinghamshire. This was going to be a big one—796 heavy bombers, Lancasters (570) and Halifaxes (226), were to take part.

The news stung the scores of operational bomber stations scattered between Colchester in the south of England and Middlesbrough in the north into intense activity. It meant many hours of back-breaking toil for the ground crews. A colossal loading job was necessary before an operation of this size. Between them the 796 bombers devoured 1.5 million gallons of high-octane aviation fuel, 37,000 gallons of lubricating oil, more than 2,700 tons of bombs, 14 million rounds of MG ammunition and tons of radar-confusing 'Window' foil. By any standards, a strategic bomber force was a greedy consumer of materials.

By 2130 that evening the preparations were complete.

The aircrews climbed aboard their bombers. The 5,500 men were as international a force as ever went into battle. They came from all over the British Commonwealth, from Britain itself, from Australia and Canada, from South Africa, Rhodesia and New Zealand. Others had escaped from countries still under the Nazi heel: from Czechoslovakia, Poland and France, from Belgium, Holland and Norway.

Soon the evening darkness shrouding the bomber airfields was shattered as aero engines coughed into life. One by one, bombers rolled off the dispersal points, to take their places in the queue for the runway. At 2200 there was a green 'Clear-to-take-off' signal from the control towers. The first of the bombers trundled noisily down the runways. At a speed of a little over 100 mph, the heavily-laden machines lifted clumsily off the ground into the dark sky.

Once airborne the bombers gained height and curved round to a SE heading. They moved in an untidy swarm—like bees. As each plane left the British coast behind the bomb-aimer flicked a switch to arm the bombs. If released now, they would explode on impact. Short test bursts were fired on the .303in Browning guns. Then the crews settled down to what they hoped might be an uneventful ride to the target and back.

Out over the North Sea the climbing bombers converged from a shapeless mass into a carefully pre-arranged pattern. At the head of the force were the pathfinder aircraft, crewed by the more experienced members of RAF Bomber Command and equipped with the latest aids to navigation. These machines were loaded with special target-indicator bombs, and their crews were to mark out Nuremberg for the five separate waves of laden bombers following close behind.

The British tactics were to route the bombers to and from the target in a tight mass. In the case of the Nuremberg attack the 796 bombers were planned to occupy an area of sky about 65 miles long, 10 miles wide and about 5,000ft—

◁◁ *Lancaster B111 PG-S had two engines put out of action over Nuremberg. Sgt. Pilot J. Parker coaxed it back to England, where it crashed and burned out. Parker and his crew were killed on a later raid.*
◁ *Bombing-up a Lancaster of Australian 463 Sqdn, flown over Nuremberg by Flying Officer Joe Foster.*
▽ *Crews of 51 Sqdn being briefed for the Nuremberg raid. Thirty-five of them were killed over the German city.*
▽▽ *Me 110 pilots of 1* Gruppe, Nachtjagdgeschwader *4, being briefed on weather conditions just before the raid.*

one mile—deep, a thundering phalanx of machinery moving forwards at $3\frac{3}{4}$ miles per minute. This was the so-called 'bomber stream', a tactic which had served the RAF well during scores of battles in the past. It meant that each line of the German defenses could be saturated in turn, by the sheer profusion of targets: an average of 40 bombers a minute passed any given point on the ground below.

Although 795 out of the planned 796 bombers had got airborne, 85 aircraft returned to their bases soon afterwards with one part or other of the complex bombing machinery failing to respond as it should.

But even before the first of the bombers had crossed the coast of England, the Germans had their eyes on them.

The fact that there was to be an attack by Bomber Command that night came as no surprise to *Generalmajor* Wolfgang Martini's *Luftwaffe* Signals Service. By a thorough study of the deliberately feeble ground-test transmissions from RAF bombers, Martini's men were able to predict the imminence of raids with a fair degree of accuracy. Heavy test traffic in the morning, and very little in the afternoon (when the aircraft were being bombed-up and refuelled) was a fair indication that a mass attack was imminent. If no attack had been planned by the RAF the day's test transmissions were evenly spread over both morning and afternoon. On the morning of 30 March the air had been thick with test transmissions, while in the afternoon very little had been heard. At 1700 Martini's staff passed warning of the expected attack to *Generaloberst* Hans-Juergen Stumpff's Reich Air Defence Headquarters at Berlin-Wannsee.

The listening service's forecast had been confirmed shortly before 2300 as the vanguard of the attacking force had risen above the horizon of the early warning radar stations situated on the coasts of Belgium and Holland. Then the stations had begun to report increasingly severe jamming on their screens. Almost immediately the German night fighter commander, *Generalmajor* Josef Schmidt, ordered his immediate-readiness fighters to scramble, even though the majority of the British bomber force had yet to cross the British coast. This early take-off was important. The cruising speed of the German night fighters was not much higher than that of the bombers they were to engage. And the distance from the bomber bases in Cambridgeshire to the Ruhr is no more than the distance from the outlying fighter bases in Southern Denmark or Berlin to the Ruhr. It was therefore vital to concentrate some of the defending fighters in the west as soon as possible, if they were to cover targets in Western Germany.

As the night fighters hastened to their radio assembly beacons, the British radio-jamming organization made its presence felt. Powerful transmitters in England beamed out a raucous cacophony on the German fighters' radio channels. Some of the bombers—specially equipped for the task—joined in. Together they caused considerable confusion, as the war diarist of the German night fighter force noted: '*Korps* VHF jammed by bell sounds, R/T traffic hardly possible, jamming of *Korps* HF by quotations from the Fuehrer's speeches, *Korps* alternative frequency strongly jammed . . . .'

But, the electronic battle that night was not going to be one-sided. The Germans were also well-equipped in this field. More important, they had kept secret from British Intelligence service three devices just introduced into service.

Since late autumn 1943 the *Luftwaffe* had been busily re-equipping its night fighters with a new radar set, the *SN-2*. The significance of the *SN-2* was that it was not vulnerable to the swamping effect of the 'Window' foil carried by the attacking bombers, as its predecessor had been. But this immunity would remain intact only so long as the device could be kept secret. The Germans had gone to great lengths to hide the details of *SN-2* from their enemies. When a night-fighter fitted with the radar had forced-landed near Zurich earlier in the year, the Swiss government were made a present of 12 examples of the latest version of the day-fighting Messerschmitt 109, for turning a blind eye when the night-fighter had 'mysteriously' exploded.

Bombers pin-pointed themselves

The other two secret devices, *Naxburg* and *Korfu*, made use of the radar signals from the bombers themselves. For accurate navigation, and to find their targets in bad weather or through cloud, the British pathfinder aircraft had to rely on their H2S radar sets. H2S gave a picture of the ground over which the aircraft was passing, 'painting' built-up areas brightly, open countryside less brightly, and the sea or areas covered by water hardly at all. It was the highly-distinctive H2S signals that the *Naxburg* and *Korfu* ground direction-finding stations picked up, and traced to their sources. The information from these two German devices was extremely valuable on three counts. First, because as the distinctive signals could only come from H2S-equipped aircraft, there was no difficulty in identifying friend from foe—as was often the case with conventional radar detection. Second, the two devices were unjammable—unless the RAF chose to transmit jamming on its own frequencies. Third, and most important of all, the devices gave a clear indication of the positions of the British pathfinders which headed the bomber streams.

This last attribute was particularly useful to the German raid-tracking service as the Nuremberg attack developed. The diversion raids by high-flying Mosquito light bombers to Cologne, Kassel and Frankfurt were all recognised as such early on: the Mosquitoes used did not carry H2S.

Earlier in the day the RAF forecasters had experienced great difficulty in predicting the state of the weather over Germany at the time of the raid. The overall pattern was highly changeable. They felt, however, that the balance of probabilities was that during that night there would be fairly good cloud cover at high level, clearing just short of the target to give good visibility over Nuremberg, with a wind of about 60 knots from the NW. Had this tentative forecast been confirmed by reality, the bomber crews would have enjoyed reasonable attacking conditions. But it was not to be.

The leading bombers crossed the Belgian/German border just before midnight; weather conditions were far from ideal. Instead of the expected cloud cover during the approach flight there were only a few puffs. Even these were

about 7,000ft below the bombers. Moreover, the expected NW wind of 60 knots turned out to be somewhat variable in strength and more from the west. Some crews later reported that they had measured winds of over 90 knots coming from the *south*. The result of all this was that the planned concentrated bomber stream was beginning to break up: soon the bombers covered an area 40 miles wide and more than 120 miles long—four times that which had been planned. The lack of cloud cover had been bad enough. But this combined with the unexpected winds did not augur well for the raiding force. It was the third unpredicted weather phenomenon which finally spelt disaster for the bombers.

Each minute, the petrol burned in each of the bombers' engines produced approximately one gallon of water in the form of steam. In normal temperatures this stream dispersed. But on this very cold night it condensed, and long white condensation trails of vapor began to chase remorselessly behind the bombers—a rare phenomenon at the 20,000ft altitude of the raiders. It was a clear night, and the glow of the half-full moon gave the vapor trails a phosphorescent quality which could be seen from great distances: the bombers were losing their cloak of invisibility.

Ex-Battle of Britain pilot *Generalmajor* Walther Grabmann, commander of the German 3rd Fighter Division across whose area the bombers were now passing, had collected his fighters over assembly beacon 'Ida', just south of Aachen. Grabmann had intended to hold them there until the bombers' route was clear to him and he could direct them into the stream. But is was soon obvious that no further directions were necessary for the fighters orbiting 'Ida': the bomber stream, widened out by the unexpected winds, was now bearing down upon the beacon itself.

German fighter tactics

Oberst (Colonel) Hajo Herrmann, one of the German fighter area commanders that night, remembers: 'There were two pieces of information I had to get from my fighters before they went into action against the bomber stream. First, the location of the bombers. Second, the direction in which the bombers were flying. This had to be radioed back to HQ *before* the attack was made. If the night fighter crew waited until afterwards, the bomber's evasive manoeuvres might have drawn them well clear of the bomber stream and heading in any direction.' Now, the ether was thick with position reports and *Pauke!* calls. *Pauke!*, *Luftwaffe* equivalent to the RAF's 'Tally Ho!', meant that the crew had made contact with the enemy and was about to engage.

The bombers tossed out 'Window' by the thousand bundles. But although the metal foil effectively neutralized the flak-control radar sets on the ground, it scarcely showed at all on the screens of the new *SN-2* radars carried by most of the night fighters.

Thus began a running battle which lasted for more than 200 miles. Bob Truman remembers: 'We saw a tremendous amount of activity, with scores of bombers going down and much air-to-air firing.' Flying Officer George Foley, who flew as a radar operator on one of the pathfinder aircraft, later recalled that he knew that things were beginning to go badly when he heard his pilot say: 'Better put your parachutes on, chaps. I have just seen the 42nd go down.' And Lancaster pilot Flight Lieutenant Graham Ross's feelings were those of many another bomber captain: 'I was very shaken at seeing so many aircraft going down in flames. I was scared by that, but still more scared

1 Generalmajor *Schmidt* (*center*) *commander of the German night-fighter force in March 1944.*
2 *Loading a 4,000lb 'cookie' into a Mosquito of 692 Sqdn. based at Graveley, Hunts. The thin-skinned bomb was designed for blast-effect, damaging structures so that following incendiary attacks would be successful.*
3 *'Window' foil being released from a Lancaster. The thin metallic strips effectively blocked radar systems plotting bomber tracks. For the Nuremberg raid tons of 'Window' were scattered by the bombers.*
4 *The moment of release. A bomb-aimer's thumb poised over the button of a Mk IX bomb-sight mounted in a Lancaster.*

A. Price

4

M. Middlebrook/J. Gover

Imperial War Museum

Imperial War Museum

at the thought that my own crew might be scared by it all.'

With the fighters which had joined the bomber stream over 'Ida' was a special *Luftwaffe* 'illuminating' unit, and these aircraft unloaded strings of parachute flares high over the bombers. These flares were spotted by fighters scores of miles away, and they converged on them like moths to a flame. The 2nd Fighter Division arrived from North Germany, the 1st came in from the Berlin area, and the 7th came in from the south. It was an ideal night for the type of fighting the German crews had been trained for, and the night fighters wrought fearful retribution on the bomber force.

Because of the scattering effect of the wind and the wide spread of the raiding force, the German fighter controllers had great difficulty in determining which target the bombers were making for. But if there was doubt as to where the raiders were going, there could be none on where they had been. The bombers' track from 'Ida' eastwards was clearly marked by the trail of wrecked aircraft burning on the ground. Not until 0108, just two minutes before the first of the bombs were due to fall on Nuremberg, was the city mentioned in the German fighters' radio broadcasts.

As the bombers approached Nuremberg the cloud conditions were found to be exactly the opposite to those forecast. Instead of cloud cover *en route*, clearing before the target was reached, there were clear skies until the target area, when the cloud began to build up. Over the city itself there was almost complete cloud cover, extending up to 17,000ft. As the pathfinders released their markers—parachute-supported flares glowing red and giving off yellow stars—they either vanished into the murk or else were carried away to the east by the wind. The result was that the attack was ineffective, the bombs scattered over a wide area.

Margin between success and failure

Due to the persistent harassment by the German night-fighters and the high cloud over the target, the actual attack on Nuremberg was scattered and diffuse. The few bombs that hit the city fell on the NE quarter. The town of Lauf, six miles to the east, suffered some damage as did several small villages in the area. But for the most part the hundreds of tons of incendiary and high-explosive bombs expended their venom harmlessly over the open fields. The main industrial section of Nuremberg, in the SW, was virtually unscathed. Strategically, such a result would have been poor even for a small-scale raid. That it was all there was to show for a maximum-effort attack which at the outset involved 796 heavy bombers illustrates, in the starkest terms, the narrow margin that separated a successful air attack from one that was an abject failure.

Defending Nuremberg were the 88mm AA guns of *Oberst* Wilhelm Juergens's 93rd *Flak* Regiment. But Juergens was able to achieve little; *his* fire-control radars were not immune to the British 'Window' jamming, and *his* searchlights could not penetrate the clouds any better than could the glow from the raiders' markers. Moreover, Juergens had to restrict his fire to targets below 20,000ft because of the presence of German night fighters overhead.

One of the bombers badly mauled by fighters, 70 miles from Nuremberg during the final run-in to the target, was a Halifax LK797 'Excalibur' of No. 578 Squadron, piloted by 22-year-old Pilot Officer Cyril J. Barton. First a Junkers 88 scored several hits. One of these smashed the aircraft's intercom system. Then a Messerschmitt joined in and its fire damaged an engine, holing two fuel tanks, and shot away the three gun turrets' hydraulic system so that there could be no return fire. Only a series of violent 'corkscrew' evasive maneuvers by Barton prevented the final destruction of the Halifax, and the fighters were at last shaken off. While all this was going on there was considerable confusion on board because conversation between the crew members was impossible. A mis-interpreted light signal from Barton was taken as being the 'bale out' order. The navigator, bomb aimer and wireless operator promptly abandoned the plane. Undeterred by losing half his crew in this way, Barton held his battered bomber on course towards Nuremberg. On arrival at the target area he picked one of the scattered parachute markers and released his 588 tiny incendiary bombs on it, before finally swinging his plane westwards.

As the widely-dispersed bomber force withdrew from the target area, the hounding night fighters began to lose contact. At least the surviving bombers could make their return flights unmolested.

Barton's Halifax was one of those bombers limping back home. The damaged motor was out of balance, and as the airscrew rotated the whole aircraft shuddered in sympathy. Suddenly there was a loud bang, and the propellor tore itself from its shaft and fell into the gloom. Barton's troubles were not over yet. Fuel was streaming out of the two holed fuel tanks. It was even money on whether the crippled Halifax would ever make it back home.

Pilot's posthumous VC

Barton did succeed in nursing his battered machine over the coast. But by this time the bomber was very low indeed. Then, while he was looking for an airfield on which to land, the fuel finally ran out. Immediately, two of the three remaining engines cut. The bomber began to dive. With not enough altitude for the remaining crew members to bail out with any degree of safety, the pilot ordered them to their crash-landing stations and tried to set the Halifax down in a field. Even in this his luck deserted him. As he lined himself up houses loomed out of the darkness. He was forced to waste some of his precious air speed in an effort to avoid them. The Halifax went out of control and struck the ground with great force. The crew members, braced in their crash-landing positions, survived the impact but Barton, who had remained at his post until the end, was killed. Cyril Barton was awarded a posthumous Victoria Cross. 'Excalibur' was the 107th victim of the Nuremberg raid and it had been her crew's 18th mission.

Bombers landed on the coastal airfields with all manner of damage. Flight Sergeant Reinell, of the Canadian No. 433 (Porcupine) Squadron flew his Halifax for nearly two hours with a raging fire in the starboard wing. After he had landed at Manston in Kent, 32sq ft of the wing's aluminium skinning had been burnt away.

Forty-eight heavy bombers landed at airfields in England with damage, many of them hit so badly that they were fit only for the scrap heap. Far worse was the number of those which did not return at all. At first the bases did not worry too much. Aircraft often landed at other airfields damaged or short of fuel. Then, as the details of these arrivals and those aircraft which had crashed on British soil became known, there still remained ominous gaps in the lists of those who had set out less than 12 hours earlier. As the day wore on the magnitude of the disaster became clear: 94 of the Nuremberg raiders failed to return, as did one aircraft engaged in dropping supplies to the French Resistance. More than 600 men were unaccounted for. Most of these

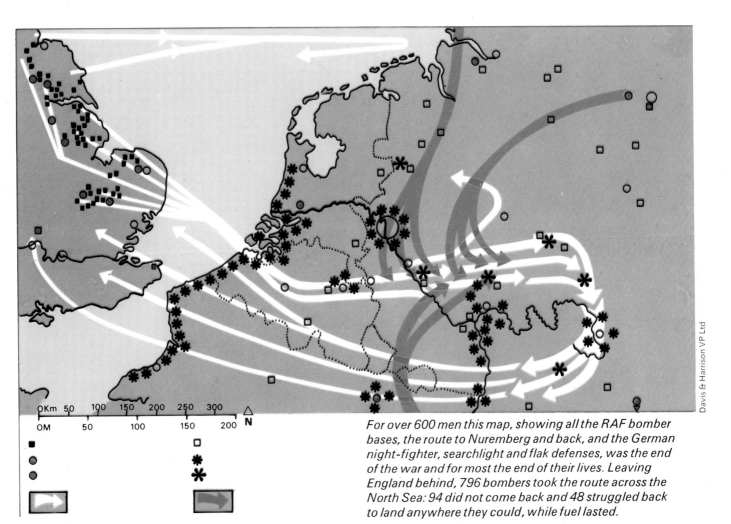

Davis & Harrison VP Ltd

0 Km 50   100   150   200   250   300
OM   50   100   150   200   N

For over 600 men this map, showing all the RAF bomber bases, the route to Nuremberg and back, and the German night-fighter, searchlight and flak defenses, was the end of the war and for most the end of their lives. Leaving England behind, 796 bombers took the route across the North Sea: 94 did not come back and 48 struggled back to land anywhere they could, while fuel lasted.

A. Price/I.W.M.

△ Pilot Officer J. Barton took Halifax LK797 over Nuremberg after being badly hit by enemy action. He pressed on to release his load of 4lb incendiaries. He got the crippled bomber back but was killed as he made a crash landing in the north of England. He was awarded a posthumous VC for 'unsurpassed courage and devotion to duty'.
▷ A Lancaster of 101 Sqdn scatters its load of 4lb incendiary bombs.

M. Middlebrook/I.W.M.

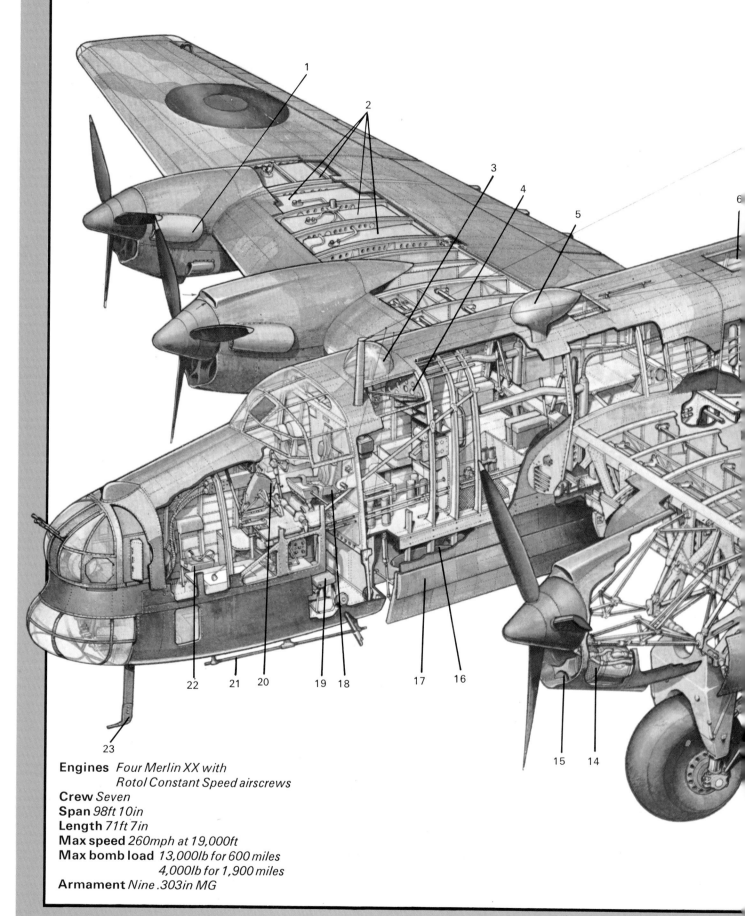

Engines *Four Merlin XX with*
Rotol Constant Speed airscrews
Crew *Seven*
Span *98ft 10in*
Length *71ft 7in*
Max speed *260mph at 19,000ft*
Max bomb load *13,000lb for 600 miles*
4,000lb for 1,900 miles
Armament *Nine .303in MG*

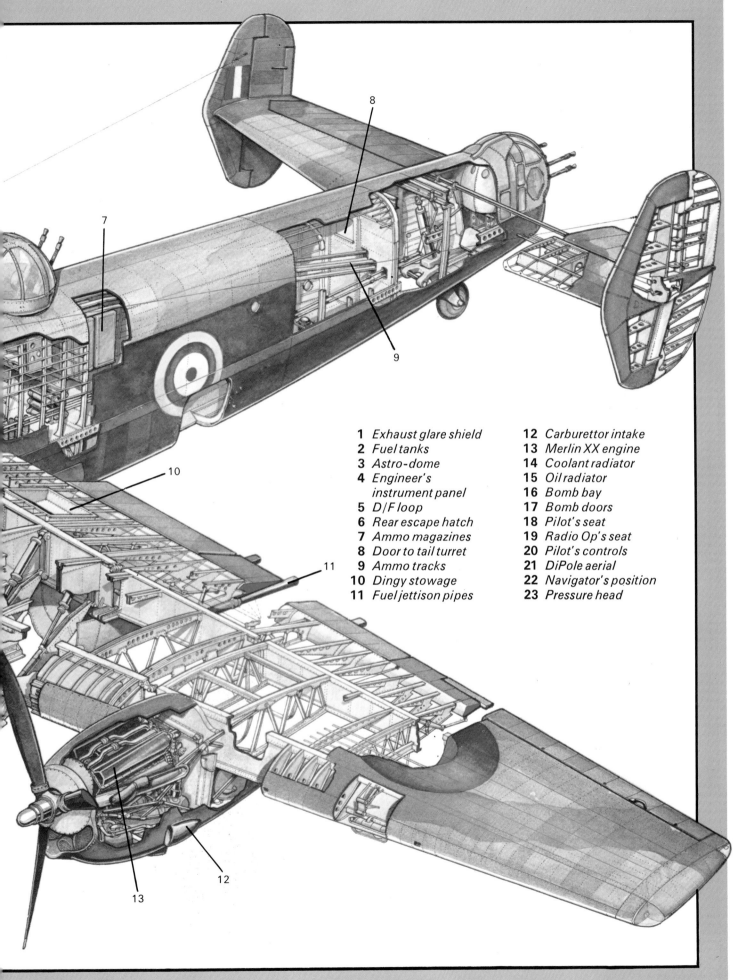

1 Exhaust glare shield
2 Fuel tanks
3 Astro-dome
4 Engineer's instrument panel
5 D/F loop
6 Rear escape hatch
7 Ammo magazines
8 Door to tail turret
9 Ammo tracks
10 Dingy stowage
11 Fuel jettison pipes
12 Carburettor intake
13 Merlin XX engine
14 Coolant radiator
15 Oil radiator
16 Bomb bay
17 Bomb doors
18 Pilot's seat
19 Radio Op's seat
20 Pilot's controls
21 DiPole aerial
22 Navigator's position
23 Pressure head

were already dead. Of the survivors, the majority were soon captured by the Germans.

The loss rate, nearly 13 per cent of the aircraft which had taken off destroyed, was not in fact the greatest proportional loss suffered by a raiding force during World War II. During smaller attacks there were scores of occasions when losses were suffered which proportionally were far higher: for example during its attempts to stem part of the German advance through France, on 17 May 1940, No. 82 Squadron, RAF, lost 11 out of the 12 Blenheim medium bombers committed and the surviving aircraft was severely damaged. This represented a loss rate of 91.6 per cent. Nor did the total of 107 aircraft destroyed represent the greatest numerical loss during a single day's action. During the so-called 'Marianas Turkey Shoot' battle fought between Japanese and US Navy aircraft near Guam in the Pacific on 19 June 1944, the Japanese lost 243 aircraft out of 373 committed—a loss rate of 65 per cent. The Nuremberg raid did, however, see the greatest *numerical* loss of *four-engined heavy bombers* ever suffered *during a single action*. During each of the two Schweinfurt battles in late 1943 the Americans lost 60 heavy bombers (though on each occasion their raiding forces comprised less than half the number of aircraft committed against Nuremberg, so the *proportional* loss was higher than that suffered by RAF Bomber Command).

Throughout Saturday 31 March, Dr Joseph Goebbels' propaganda services broadcast the news of the victory. By 1944 such opportunities were rare, so they made the most of this one: *Announcement: we have just received news of a great new success of our air defences in the battle against the British terror formations. Last night our night fighters, with the AA guns, inflicted the heaviest defeat so far on the British air formations. According to reports so far received, at least 132 four-engined bombers were destroyed over western or southern Germany.*

The German defenses were naturally elated by their success. As one of those involved in the action, *Oberleutnant* Fritz Brandt later recalled: 'It was possible to plot your course to the target by the number of wrecked aircraft which we could see the next day. They ran in a smouldering line across half of Germany.' Initial reports stated that 132 of the bombers had been shot down. Later, after many of the duplicated claims were weeded out, this figure was reduced to 101 with 6 'probables'. That night the German night-fighter force lost five aircraft destroyed and five more damaged beyond repair. Three crewmen were killed, one was wounded and eight missing.

It was the climax of the German efforts to defend their homeland against the night raiders but, ironically, it was virtually the last time they were able to do so with any great success. The circumstances, which had combined to bring about such ideal conditions for night fighting were never to be repeated. For the bombers, the weather had been 'exceptionally bad'. And, by definition, exceptional conditions are very rare. Thus far *SN-2*, *Naxburg* and *Korfu* had escaped the notice of the ever-vigilant British Intelligence service; but their secrets were not kept for much longer. One by one they were discovered. Retribution was swift. To counter *SN-2* the RAF introduced a new, long-cut version of 'Window' which effectively swamped the radar screens with false targets; to counter *Naxburg* and *Korfu*, the bombers' radar operators changed to tactics which made ground direction-finding impossible until the target area was reached.

After the Nuremberg disaster there were widespread rumors in Bomber Command that treachery had been the cause, that 'somebody had talked'. This notion is not supported by examination of the *Luftwaffe* records. Moreover, if the Germans had known beforehand that the target was to be Nuremberg, why was it that the night fighters had fought the main battle *en route* to the target, and lost contact with the bombers almost immediately after it? What were the short-range fighters doing orbiting beacons uselessly remote from the battle area?

The truth was that in the early months of 1944 the German night fighter force could be likened to a powerfully-built but short-sighted prize fighter, furiously swinging a leaden fist. On Black Friday in March 1944 that fist had connected.   **Alfred Price**

Although a disastrous raid for the RAF, some bombs did hit Nuremberg. The Aiming Point was the Alstadt and residential area. Here, only 500 yards from the Aiming Point, can be seen the wreckage of a police station.

Surrounded by the inevitable crowd of ghouls who gather at every unpleasant accident, the broken body of an RAF man lies where it fell after his parachute failed him. His pockets are being searched for identification papers.

'BIG WEEK' 1944

Allied airfleets are poised to batter Germany into rubble. Could the weakening Luftwaffe beat the big bombers?

P51 Mustangs escort B24J Liberators of 458th Bomb Group over Europe. Close attendance was due to the top secret Azon radio-controlled 1,000lb bomb, three of which were carried. Just visible is the rear-set triple aerial array on 'J4'.

Since November 1943, dense cloud in the winter skies over NW Europe had hidden Nazi Germany beneath a protective blanket. But as the days lengthened in February 1944 the cloud began to thin. At the British bases of the US 8th Air Force the heavy bombers were fuelled and armed. They would soon strike deep into the heart of the Reich once more.

Across the North Sea the *Luftwaffe* fighter squadrons were also preparing for battle. The Nazis knew only too well that with clear skies the Fortresses and Liberators, accompanied by their aggressive fighter escorts, would attack in force—their target, the German fighter factories.

On 19 February, 1944, Allied weather reports indicated good visibility over Germany. The 8th Air Force was alerted for action. As the long white contrails threw their ribbons across the North Sea, *Luftwaffe* fighters scrambled to intercept. The world's two mightiest air armadas were about to clash in mortal combat four miles above Nazi-dominated Europe.

In the three weeks following some of the most ferocious air battles ever fought took place in the skies over Germany. These clashes virtually decided which side was to command the air over the western front and sealed the fate of the Third Reich. How did the aircraft of the combatants measure up to each other? What tactics did the Allies and the Germans employ to make the most use of their planes?

Backbone of the US 8th Air Force's strategic bomber force was the Boeing B17 Fortress. This formidable machine

equipped 20 bombardment groups by the early months of 1944. From September onwards the B17G variant was reaching combat squadrons. The most conspicuous feature of this plane was the chin turret below the glazed nose which housed a pair of .50s. (Later examples of the earlier B17F were also fitted with this turret.) Nine groups of the 8th had B24 Liberators, a bomber with a very high aspect ratio (narrow) wing that gave it a higher wing-loading than the B17 and made it rather heavy on the controls with a tendency to fall away violently in propeller wash. To make up for this relatively poor stability, the B24 cruised about 20mph faster than the B17, had a longer range, and carried more bombs. But the differing flight characteristics of these two bombers made mixed flight formations impractical. At the beginning of 1944 the B24H entered service. This model had a nose turret which increased the overall weight and reduced the speed, resulting in less responsive controls. The nose was also very draughty due to insufficient padding around the new turret. The Liberator was never as popular in Europe as in the Middle East or the Pacific, and it gained a reputation for catching fire too easily when damaged.

The Americans relied on the P47D Thunderbolt for escort. This big, heavy fighter carried 500 gallons of fuel (200 in a drop tank) but its thirsty radial engine consumed 100 gallons of high octane an hour—limiting the range to 835 miles. The P47 had tremendous diving speed, a very high ceiling of 42,000ft, and a good rate of roll that made it extremely maneuverable at altitude. It could also withstand considerable battle damage, and delivered a formidable weight of firepower from its eight .50 MGs, but its rate of climb was not good and below 15,000ft it compared unfavorably with German fighters.

Much had been expected of the P38 Lightning which equipped a small number of groups in England, but this unorthodox twin-engined single-seater was not a spectacular success in NW Europe. It was certainly fast, and the P38J variant had a useful combat radius of 640 miles. But above 20,000ft the Allison engines suffered from sluggish oil that refused to flow properly in the intense cold of high altitude, leading to heavy oil consumption, an engine life of only 80 hours, and frequently to mechanical failure. The turbo-superchargers were troublesome too, and P38 cockpits had such poor heating that pilots became numb with cold and frequently had to be helped out after a long mission. Below 18,000ft the Lightning was able to turn with both the Me109 and the FW190 and could also out-climb them, but above this height the P38's poor rate of roll and inferior diving speed placed it at a disadvantage. Because of these technical problems and performance deficiencies, the P38 was rarely taken above 30,000ft, which meant that the Me109s, usually cruising at around 35,000, were able to look out for the Lightnings' telltale double contrails and bounce them with impunity. P38 losses quickly became insupportable.

Mustang—superb long-range escort fighter

The full potential of the Merlin-engined P51 Mustang had not been appreciated late in 1943. Initially P51Bs and Cs were allocated to the US 9th Air Force for purely tactical use. The outstanding capability of this fighter in the long-range escort role rapidly became apparent, however, and 9th Air Force P51s were assigned to fly in support of the 8th Air Force heavy bombers. The 8th's fighter groups were given priority for re-equipment with Mustangs.

With the relatively economical liquid-cooled in-line engine and a fuel load of 419 gallons (including two 75 gallon drop tanks) the P51 had a huge combat range of 1,500 miles. It was also faster than both the Me109G and FW190A, particularly above 30,000ft, could out-dive both the German fighters (although the 109G did have better initial acceleration) and had a superior rate of climb. In a dog-fight the Mustang could easily turn with a 109, though the FW190 was probably the equal of the American plane in this kind of maneuver and it had a better rate of roll.

The RAF's contribution to the big daylight air battles of early 1944 was mainly restricted to short-range escorts. Its Spitfire IXs had been designed primarily as defensive interceptors. In close combat the Spitfire's superb handling qualities made it a match for any other fighter flying, but the two German fighters could outdive it and were consequently able to break off an engagement virtually at will.

The *Luftwaffe* had about 900 single-seater fighters to combat this formidable daylight fighting force. Germany's most feared interceptor at this time was the FW190A, a robustly built plane that was at its best flying low or at medium altitudes. Above 20,000ft the BMW engine was very troublesome, but this big radial power unit afforded the pilot considerable protection from a bomber's defensive fire and the 190's sharp acceleration and very high rate of roll made it difficult for Allied fighter pilots to catch it.

The Me109G was not an easy plane to fly, with its high wing loading, narrow-tracked undercarriage and pro-

△ Ground-crew servicing Focke-Wulf 190As lined up on a German tarmac.
▷ Bombs explode far below the starboard wing of a B17 Fortress during a daylight raid on Berlin, 29 April 1944. More than 700 'heavies' attacked the German capital on this raid with over 1,500 tons of bombs.
▽ A blazing B17 Fortress breaks up as it plunges to earth after being hit. Bombs from another fall in track down to the synthetic oil plant at Merseberg, Germany.

nounced tendency to swing during take-off and landing. But the altitude performance was good, which made it an obvious choice for sending after the high-flying American escort fighters, but an endurance of only about 55 minutes was hopelessly inadequate. Many a 109 was lost through running out of fuel during combat. In battle with Allied interceptors the Messerschmitt fared more poorly than the Focke-Wulf and 109 squadrons suffered heavy casualties, partly because they were often detailed to do battle with Mustangs and Thunderbolts.

A number of Me110 twin-engined fighters remained in service to carry out rocket attacks on bomber formations. But the vulnerability of this large and cumbersome aircraft meant that it was principally used over central and southern Germany where there was less chance of interceptions by American escort fighters. A later derivative of this design (the Me410) was used in small numbers, but proved no more effective than the original 110.

By February 1944 the US 8th Air Force was beginning to use radar for locating targets beneath dense cloud cover. It was also training elite lead crews who flew bombers equipped with every available navigation and bombing aid. These lead ships flew in the van of bomber formations and led their squadrons over the target—bombardiers being instructed to release their bombs when the lead ship unloaded.

Improving Thunderbolt performance

Efforts were made to improve the performance of the P47 by paring-off surplus weight. At the same time water injection into the inlet manifold of the big Pratt & Whitney R2800 engine gave an extra 300hp for short periods and materially improved the maximum speed and rate of climb at altitudes of up to 30,000ft, particularly when new paddle-bladed propellers were fitted.

The P51 experienced a certain amount of trouble as it climbed high into the cold, damp winter skies of NW Europe. Guns jammed if they were fired in any position other than straight and level flight, necessitating re-seating of the armament. British spark plugs had to be fitted in place of American ones, cockpit windows iced up, and problems were encountered with fuel systems and radios. The bombers also had their difficulties. A number of B17s (and occasionally B24s) were lost when damaged engines 'ran away' due to failure of the hydraulic feathering mechanism, which drew its oil from the engine itself. If the engine lost all its lubricant, the constant speed unit would not work—a defect that was not remedied until the autumn of 1944.

The *Luftwaffe* was beginning to introduce the new long-nosed FW190D, with a Junkers Jumo liquid-cooled engine. This formidable machine began operational trials with JG3 towards the end of 1943 and represented a substantial improvement over the FW190A, with a maximum speed of 426mph at 21,000ft, a high rate of climb, phenomenal acceleration at the beginning of a dive, and a very tight turning circle. It was probably the best propeller-driven fighter to see service with the *Luftwaffe* during the war.

The high-pressure area which developed over central Germany on 19 February 1944 brought with it clear skies that endured for a whole week. During this much-publicised 'Big Week' from 19 to 25 February the US 8th Air Force put up its most concentrated effort of the war so far—3,300 bomber sorties, dropping 6,000 tons of bombs on targets

49

△ Improved power enabled the F and G models of the P38 Lightning to carry more armament or drop-tanks. With a top speed of over 400mph and a range of 450 miles, it was the best long-range tactical fighter of World War II.
▷ P47 Thunderbolt of 82 Fighter Squadron, 78th Fighter Group. The engine cowling's checkerboard design was first used in April 1944. It was armed with four .5in Brownings.
▽ B17 Flying Fortress, prime instrument in the air attacks on Germany by the US 8th AAF. Protected by eight or nine .5in Browning MGs and capable of carrying a 20,000lb bomb load at short range.

ranging from Brunswick, Halberstadt and Aschersleben in the north to Stuttgart, Augsburg and Regensburg in the south.

The Germans deployed their fighters skilfully. Radar gave warning of American formations assembling over England, and a flexible organisation enabled fighters to be quickly summoned to the combat zone—sometimes from all over western Germany, Holland, Belgium and northern France.

The American fighters were often attacked as they crossed in from the North Sea to make them jettison their drop tanks—curtailing their range. Firing-passes on the bombers were usually made head-on in line abreast at *Staffel* strength as the B17s and B24s could bring fewer guns to bear straight ahead and there was also a better chance of hitting either the engines or the flight deck. German fighter pilots were ordered to pull up over the bombers so as not to lose combat altitude, but many of them half rolled and dived away on their backs instead—a less dangerous maneuver.

The bomber box occupying the lowest position in the leading wing seemed to bear the brunt of fighter attacks. This hazardous position was taken in turn by the bomber crews. The *Luftwaffe* knew well that the lead ships carried specially trained crews. These became prime targets for the fighters.

△ Pilot Bob Fuller and some of his crew lived after AA fire had ripped off the port wing of 'Wee Willie', a B17 of 91st Bomber Group.

△ ◁ A double Thunderbolt hit on a luckless Me 110. First US fighter hit the German aircraft and set its port fuel tank ablaze, when a second P47 cut in and finished the demolition job.

▽ Early models of the NA P51 Mustang did not carry the tear-drop cockpit canopy shown on this P51D. Top speed was over 420mph and its armament of six .5in Browning MGs, plus a range of 950 miles, made it an ideal fighter for escorting bombers.

The American escort flew a weaving protective pattern with maybe two squadrons of a group 3,000ft or 4,000ft above the bomber boxes. A third squadron provided top cover 2,000ft or 3,000ft higher. German interceptors had to run the gauntlet of both the top-cover escort and the lower echelons of US fighters before reaching their prey—the bombers. The formidable armament of the B17s and B24s made them a dangerous adversary providing the close-formation boxes were not broken up. It was to achieve just this that rocket firing Me110s and (in small numbers) FW190As were sent in.

The German priority was to destroy the bombers. To this end their fighters were equipped with more and more cannon guns at the expense of MGs. But this relatively slow-firing armament placed them at a disadvantage in combat with Allied fighters. In a dogfight a fighter pilot is only likely to have his opponent in his sights for seconds and a heavy fusillade of quick-firing machine guns is more likely to inflict damage on another fighter than a handful of cannon shells. Compared to the 100 rounds which left a P47's guns in a one-second burst and the 80 that a P51 discharged, an FW190 fired only 60 rounds and a Me109G a mere 30.

After a week of almost continuous combat over Europe,

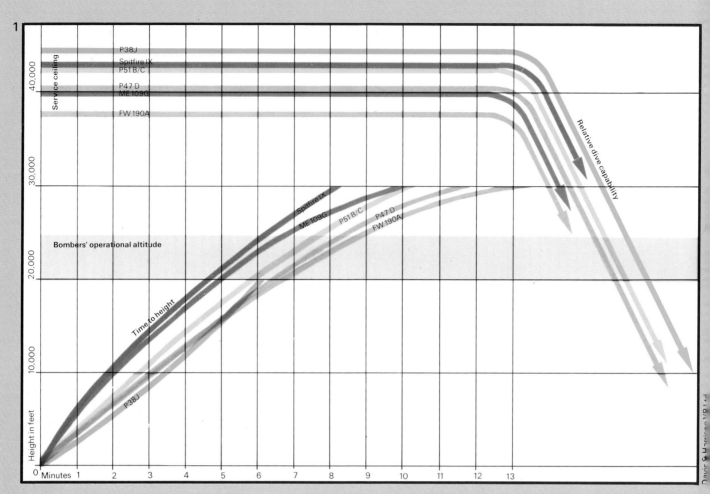

1 Graph showing relative dive capability and time-to-height. Curves labelled P38J, Spitfire IX, P51 B/C, P47 D, ME 109G, FW 190A against "Service ceiling", "Bombers' operational altitude", with axes "Height in feet" and "Minutes" (0–13), and an arrow marked "Relative dive capability".

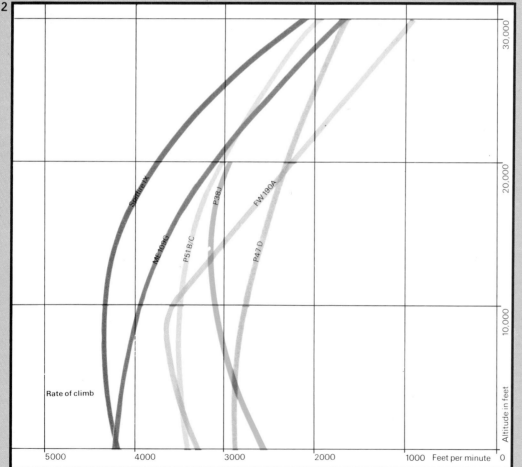

2 Graph showing rate of climb. Curves labelled Spitfire IX, ME 109G, P51 B/C, P38J, P47 D, FW 190A, with axes "Altitude in feet" (10,000–30,000) and "Feet per minute" (5000–0).

1 *During World War II opposing aircraft designers were often close to achieving parity of performance between the various types. This graph illustrates relative dive capabilities and time-to-height figures of the Allied and Luftwaffe fighters.*

2 *The Spitfire's rate of climb gave it superiority over all other fighters. Noticeable is the sharp drop-off in climb by the otherwise very effective FW190A.*

3 *Comparative ranges of British and US bombers and their long-range fighter escorts.*

4 *A B17 cameraman caught this Me 410 as it peeled away to starboard after attacking. Protruding from the nose is the formidable 50mm BK5 cannon.*

5 *A simplified airspeed indicator showing the top speeds of Allied and German fighters.*

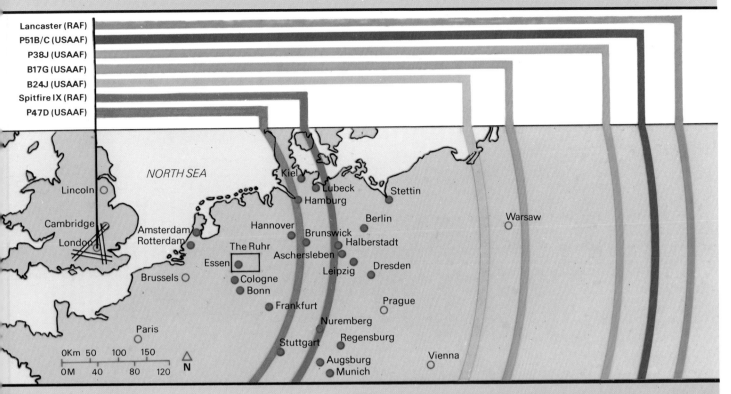

Lancaster (RAF)
P51B/C (USAAF)
P38J (USAAF)
B17G (USAAF)
B24J (USAAF)
Spitfire IX (RAF)
P47D (USAAF)

NORTH SEA

Lincoln
Cambridge
London
Amsterdam
Rotterdam
Brussels
Essen
The Ruhr
Cologne
Bonn
Paris
Frankfurt
Stuttgart
Augsburg
Munich
Hannover
Brunswick
Aschersleben
Leipzig
Nuremberg
Regensburg
Kiel
Lübeck
Hamburg
Halberstadt
Dresden
Prague
Vienna
Berlin
Stettin
Warsaw

0Km 50 100 150
0M 40 80 120
N

Imperial War Museum

the USAAF had lost 261 bombers (half of them to the *Luftwaffe*) and 33 fighters. The 8th Air Force earned no fewer than three Medals of Honor and four Distinguished Unit Citations. But the real losses inflicted on the German fighters were probably less than the claims of the American air gunners and fighter pilots. Among those who did not return, however, was *Oberstleutnant* (Lieutenant-Colonel) Egon Mayer, the *Kommodore* of JG2. He was credited with 102 victories and had instigated the use of head-on attacks against the American bomber formations. The 'Big Week' raids had, as has been mentioned, been aimed primarily at the German aircraft industry. Although some loss in production was suffered the dispersal of manufacturing facilities that the Germans had achieved since autumn 1943 made the attacks less effective than the Allies hoped.

Only a week after the huge air battles of late February the 8th Air Force attacked 'Big B' (Berlin), by daylight. A small force got through to the German capital on 4 March, but the first mass raid to hit Berlin was on 6 March, when 730 bombers set out from England at first light with an escort of 800 fighters.

The *Luftwaffe* put up 400 interceptors—nearly half of its available strength in the west. American fighter pilots claimed to have knocked down 81 for the loss of 11 US fighters. But the bombers took a severe mauling and 80 of them never returned to England.

And yet the American Fortresses and Liberators returned to Berlin 600 strong only 36 hours later. All the valiant efforts of the German fighter pilots could not stem the overwhelming tide of the American onslaught.

Mustangs could now escort the bombers all the way to Berlin and back, and new P51Ds were soon to start arriving. In this model most of the problems encountered with early P51Bs and Cs had been solved and the Mustang was to prove perhaps the finest interceptor to fly during World War II, although the *Luftwaffe* considered it to be rather vulnerable to cannon fire. The modified water-injection Thunderbolts with paddle-bladed propellers

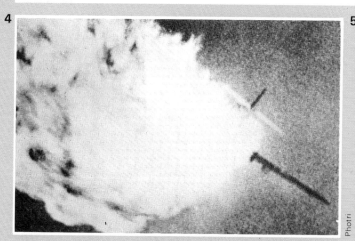

Spitfire IX — 22½lb

ME 109G — 37lb

P51 B/C — 15lb

P47 D — 20lb

FW 190A — 37lb

P38J — 19lb

Davis & Harrison VP Ltd

1 *His limbs flailing in the slipstream, a German pilot bales-out from a crippled FW190.*
2 *A B17 flies through Me410 rocket bursts as 390th Bomb Group attacks Augsburg, 16 March 1944. Two B17s were shot down.*
3 *Firepower comparison between Allied and German fighters. Each 'shell' represents about 4lb, the weight of ammunition fired in a 3-sec burst.*
4 *Relentlessly pursued by an Allied fighter, a blazing Me 109G falls.*
5 *Still flying straight and level, but not for long. A doomed B24.*

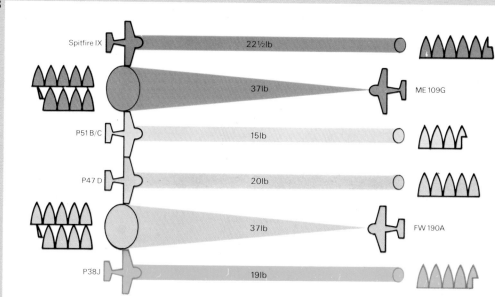

were fast enough to do battle down to ground level with the Focke-Wulfs and Messerschmitts. Below 5,000ft the FW190A still accelerated faster but the Thunderbolt could now quickly overtake it—even in a climb. Only if the speed fell below 280mph could the hitherto so formidable 190 turn inside a P47.

With increasing technical superiority the American fighters began to abandon their former defensive function and roamed far and wide seeking combat or ground strafing. The P38 Lightning never really measured up as an interceptor in Europe and was gradually phased out of service

in this role over the Western Front, but the RAF's short-range fighters moved to the Continent after the invasion so that Spitfires and the new Hawker Tempests were able to hunt the skies over Germany itself.

Neither the long-nosed Focke-Wulfs nor the belated introduction of jet and rocket fighters could save the *Luftwaffe* from annihilation in 1945. But the seeds of its defeat were originally sown during those fearful three weeks early in 1944 when winter gave way to spring and the clouds rolled back to leave the skies clear for the most savage air battles that the world has seen. **Rodney Steel**

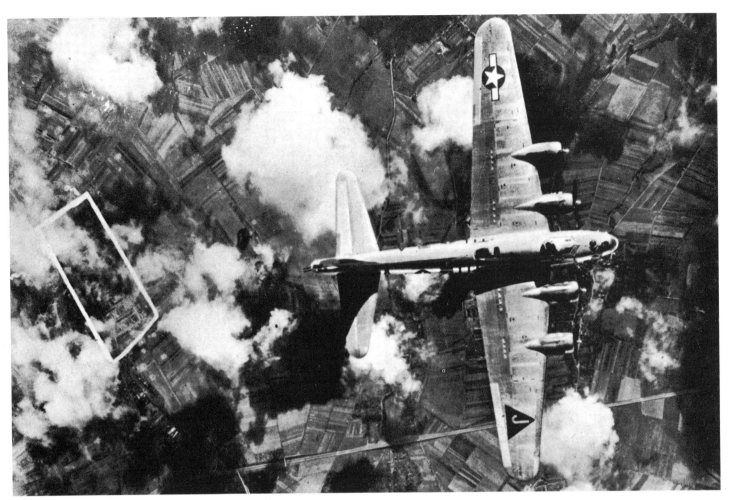

TOP: Smoke billows up from the Bettenhausen factory in Kassel as one of the attacking B-17 bombers of the U.S. 8th Air Force passes over the target area.

BELOW: A damaged Flying Fortress under repair at a Mobile Machine Shop.

W.O. Donald Gray

'BAIL OUT!'

His starboard wing ablaze, Donald Gray ordered 'Bail out!'

Sergeant Pilot Donald George Gray RAF, from Ilford, Essex, was bored with his job as an RAF Training Command staff pilot. Day after day he flew student wireless operators and air gunners round and round in an area off the west coast of Scotland and the Irish Sea while they practised radio procedure and gunnery. Later, he was appointed a classroom instructor in navigation. But Sgt. Gray wanted action. He had not joined the RAF in 1940 to act as a 'taxi' pilot or classroom teacher. His flying training had begun on the wonderful Tiger Moth, then on twin-engined Airspeed Oxfords and Avro Ansons. Unfortunately Gray's natural aptitude as a navigator was the reason for his being kept off the operational flying he so badly wanted to take part in. 'Too good a pilot for operations' was the verdict of his superiors. But Sgt. Gray had other ideas. There was

one way to get on Ops.—make yourself enough of a nuisance and a posting usually followed. So off Gray went one day to indulge in some highly improper and unauthorized low flying. For this he received an official reprimand and that sought-for posting.

The posting was to a Conversion Unit where experience of larger aircraft was gained. This time he flew Vickers Wellingtons, then the four-engined 'heavies', starting with the Short Stirling. Being such an accomplished pilot, Gray found no problems with these large bombers, the Stirling giving its usual excessive swing on take-off, but nothing more. The Lancaster he found a delight to fly, quick and responsive on controls, its four Merlins giving a much different sound from the Stirling's radial Hercules, but just as reliable.

In the spring of 1944, 22-year-old Sgt. Gray's posting to an operational unit came at last. He was given a 'headless crew'—one that had no pilot—and sent to No. 50 Squadron, based at Skellingthorpe, Lincolnshire, England, and equipped with Mk. 1 Lancasters.

After a couple of days Gray and his crew were getting to know the station and making friends. At the time he had been promoted to Warrant Officer, but the notification did not come through until later. From here on, however, he is given his proper rank.

The atmosphere on the station was far from happy. Following normal practice at Skellingthorpe, Warrant Officer Gray's crew were not allowed to leave camp for fourteen days after arrival in case the Wing Commander wanted to send them off on a cross-country flying exercise. Rigorous conversion courses to Lancasters, followed by action over Germany, meant that Gray and his crew had not any leave for about three months. On Thursday evening, 29 March, some members of the crew decided to descend on the pubs of Lincoln. Later that night, the Wing Commander wanted them for flying duties. Gray explained that some of them were out of camp and he was angrily ordered to visit every watering-hole in Lincoln and bring his wayward comrades up before his Commanding Officer.

Came the dawn of 30 March and W.O. Gray escorted the downcast miscreants of his crew to the station HQ Orderly Room to see the CO—only to be brusquely informed that the great man was planning a mission for the coming night and was far too busy to see them.

They were naturally relieved. But had they known what was in store for them, they would have willingly chosen the ogre in the office. The Wing Commander was planning Skellingthorpe's contribution to the Nuremberg Raid (30/31 March 1944).

W.O. Gray recalls a cheerful WAAF sergeant at Skellingthorpe who, it was seriously alleged, had a drastically adverse effect on the luck of her boyfriends. It was claimed that every member of the RAF she befriended failed to return from a subsequent mission. A number of RAF bomber stations also claimed a similar glamorous Gremlin. On the evening of 30 March, Gray was sitting in the Sergeant's Mess having tea when the young WAAF began chatting to him. From that moment on, knowing of the ominous tales of the girl's effect, he regarded the coming mission with gloomy forboding.

A crowd of RAF ground-staff stood near the end of the runway as W.O. Gray's Lancaster R5546 'T-for-Tare' lifted off. These people always stood there to wave the planes and their crews off and wish them 'Good Luck'. On this occasion the friendly WAAF was conspicuous in the front of the crowd.

By this stage of World War II, Gray's aircraft had been through more than 40 operations. Although well seasoned she was still reliable. Most of the flight from England to enemy territory was handled by 'George', the invaluable automatic pilot. But soon after take-off Sergeant Bert Wright, the wireless operator, found that his 'Fishpond' set was not working properly. This primitive installation warned

of other aircraft in the vicinity but could not distinguish
friend from foe. Not long after this discovery it was found
that the intercom linking the cockpit with the rear gun-
turret was faulty. There was something wrong with the
helmet of the rear gunner, Sergeant Douglas Maugham,
which also served as an oxygen mask. It seemed that the
baleful influence of the 'friendly' WAAF was again beginning to impose itself.

The W/Op took a spare helmet to the rear gunner. They
found it impossible to fix it, and Bert Wright reported that
the gunner was losing consciousness in the rarified air.

By this time, things were getting dangerous. Gray and
his crew were at 22,000ft skirting the edge of the heavy
flak defenses south of Aachen. Their lookout—the rear
gunner—was out of action. Bert Wright had to return to
his radio to be on the alert for important messages from
base. The flight engineer, Sergeant Joseph Grant, took a
portable oxygen bottle and made his way to the rear to
give assistance. Within a couple of minutes the W/Op
reported that the flight engineer, too, was unconscious
in the fuselage.

Balls of flame that were stricken bombers

'T-for-Tare' was now on course for Fulda, about 90
miles NNW of Nuremberg. Gray knew they were heading
for trouble. Ahead were the enemy fighter flares and the
massive balls of flame that were stricken bombers. Suddenly
the mid-upper gunner, Sergeant Frank Patey, shouted that
they were being attacked and began firing. Gray put the
Lancaster into evasive action—'Corkscrew Left'—until the
mid-upper AG reported the attack over, then the Lanc.
was straightened up and got back on its course of about
090 degrees.

Now there was the problem of what to do about the two
unconscious crew members. Gray had no choice but to
reduce altitude. He put down 5° of flap and began to lose
height as fast as he could without affecting ground speed.
A change in ground speed would affect his laid-down ETA
on target, and upset the calculations of Flt. Sgt. Alan
Campbell, the navigator.

Then there was an explosion.

'Christ!' screamed the bomb-aimer, Flt. Sgt. George
Wallis—'T for Tare' was hit. The starboard outer engine was
ablaze. Had the flight engineer been in his place he would
immediately have taken emergency action—petrol switched
off, pitch to coarse, props feathered—and operated the
graviner-switches which electrically set off fire extin-
guishers in the engine nacelles. As it was, Gray had to
undo his seat harness to reach the switches at the other
side of the cockpit. By the time he managed to operate
them it was too late. The starboard wing was burning
from end to end and the aircraft was in a near-vertical
dive and failing to respond. The control was jammed
firmly against the instrument panel.

Over the intercom, Gray called: 'I can't put the fire out,
and the aircraft is out of control'. There was no alternative
but to give the 'Bale out' order. Gray pressed the emergency
light button. The conscious crew members had just
acknowledged when there was another bang and Gray
felt a vicious pain sear across his left knee. Ignoring it, he
took off his gloves and helmet and clipped the parachute
pack onto his harness. Opening the bomb-doors to dump
the 4,000lb 'cookie' and the incendiaries he was faced by
dazzling light and searing heat. Then he decided not to
jettison the bomb, which would effectively destroy the

1 *A Lancaster cockpit. To the right of the wheel is the throttle quadrant, and above it the boost and rev counters for the four engines.*

2 *The Flight Engineer sitting on his fold-up seat. Below this is the step to the bomb-aimer's position down which the navigator fell just as the perspex nose of the Lancaster came away. Outlined (1) the four graviner switches which the Flight Engineer would have operated to extinguish the flames in the starboard engines. But he was still back towards the tail, and Gray had to release his seat harness in order to reach them. It was at this moment that he probably released the turnbuckle of his parachute harness.*

3 *Lancasters of 50 Sqdn, code letters VN, being bombed-up at Skellingthorpe, Lincs.*

Imperial War Museum

aircraft when it hit the ground and leave little for German Intelligence to work on. But now a mysterious object was busily slapping him about the face. It was the parachute pack. At this point W.O. Gray was convinced he had 'had it'. Realizing he had nothing to lose, he pulled the rip-cord of his parachute.

Suddenly, silence and blackness surrounded him. No heat, no flame—no aircraft. He felt nothing beyond a slight but continuous tugging at his ankles. Wondering how his arms came to be raised above his head, he lowered them. It was as if some alien force had taken charge of his body, for his arms immediately returned to the raised position. Beyond his feet was the white parachute canopy, while lights flashed in an indigo sky. And W.O. Gray realized that he was no longer a part of his blazing Lancaster. A wave of relief swept through him.

His relief turned to panic as he realized that he was hanging upside-down—a fall to certain death prevented only by the parachute harness tangled round his ankles! Gray is still not certain how his harness came to be in this position. He assumes that when he undid his seat straps to get to the graviner switches he accidentally operated the release turnbuckle on the parachute harness.

Gray locked his ankles tightly together and went through his 'limited repertoire of prayers'.

His head hit the ground

There was a gentle brushing against his face. Then his head hit the ground with a violent bang. The next thing he knew, he was flat on his back, totally winded and feeling as if every bone in his body was broken. But he was still alive.

Half-stunned and shaking, Gray stumbled to his feet.

As he moved his legs to see if any bones were broken his parachute harness dropped off. He seemed to be in one piece and could dimly make out that he was standing at the edge of a forest. He decided the best thing to do was to make himself scarce as his unusual arrival could easily have been seen.

Gray rolled up his parachute and thrust it under a bush. The white scarf around his neck was disposed of in case it gave him away in the dark. To make life difficult for any potential captors, he removed his pilot's brevet (wings) and threw it away. But Gray kept his Irvine jacket. It was a chilly night.

Making slow progress he stumbled off. His legs were badly bruised and cut about and every time he breathed there was a stabbing pain in his chest. His eye-balls felt as if they were about to burst from his head.

Silence pervaded the night. W.O. Gray listened, but could hear nothing that would lead him to any of his crew who may be alive nearby. The moon was setting in the west and Gray headed in that direction. Within a matter of seconds he stepped on to the concrete ribbon of an autobahn— a German motorway—gleaming white in the moonlight. Had he landed there Gray would have been killed outright by a broken neck.

Crossing the exposed autobahn as quickly as he could, he found himself on a footpath with park benches at intervals. This was evidently a local beauty spot. Soon he came to a road. A fast-moving stream ran beside it. There were houses nearby.

W.O. Gray was feeling pretty weary by now, so he went back up the lane and lay down under a bush to rest. But the cold of the night combined with the effects of shock

'Flight'

began to get the better of him. He began to shiver violently. Sleeping in the open would be impossible.

Suddenly, he heard the faint rumble of a train. Still in a confused state, Gray made off in the direction of the noise with the rather impractical plan of hitching a lift. On his way, the houses grew in number, and it soon became clear that he was entering a small town. A level crossing appeared in front of him.

Gray started to walk towards it. Two torches pricked the darkness near the crossing. Too tired to turn back, Gray decided to walk past on the other side of the road as inconspicuously as possible and chance that he would not be noticed.

It was a vain hope.

Four elderly civilians armed with rifles stepped out of the gloom. They all wore armbands. They were obviously the German equivalent of the British 'Home Guard'. Even though W.O. Gray was unarmed and too weak to resist, he could not help noticing that all four were terrified of him.

None of Gray's captors spoke English, but one of them could speak French. That was no help at all—Gray's schoolboy French was too rusty.

'*Americanisch?*' inquired one of his ageing captors.

'*Nein. Englander!*' Gray replied in a tone of offended patriotism.

'*Ach! Heil Churchill?*'

'*Ja!*'

He was then escorted a little way down the road, through a door, up a flight of stairs and into a neat, well-furnished office. Hitler's portrait hung on a wall. Then a policeman stalked into the room and, for some mysterious reason, began to scream and rave at Gray's bewildered, civilian captors.

His watch had stopped at 0025

But the policeman's attitude became more civil when he turned and indicated that Gray was to turn his pockets out and produce his identity discs. It was then that the Warrant Officer noticed that his watch read 0025. The impact of his landing must have stopped it.

After being given a glass of water—for which he remembered the German name '*wasser*' from a Humphrey Bogart film—and allowed to smoke one of his cigarettes, his left leg was bandaged by the policeman. It was pretty badly cut and had a nasty gash at the side of the knee.

Gray was now led downstairs, across a courtyard and into a cell. The door slammed behind him and he found himself alone in a sparsely furnished cubicle. In the corner was a roughly fashioned wooden bed with a coarse blanket thrown across it. Now, Gray felt the oppression of captivity for the first time. As he lay down, fatigue overwhelmed him. In seconds, he was asleep.

He awoke to a brilliantly sunny morning. The policeman of the night before came for him. An open lorry was parked in the yard. A knot of women and children stood staring.

Gray clambered into the back of the truck and found himself sitting next to a man wearing an RAF tunic. He was the very picture of misery and when Gray attempted to open a conversation, he was rewarded with a grunt. And Gray did not feel in the best of health either. His eyes were not swollen any more, but his legs were painfully stiff and the rest of his body felt 'as if I had been kicked by a mule'. (An investigation after the war by author Martin Middle-

brook revealed that the man was Warrant Officer Hall, RNZAF, a bomb aimer. He had been badly beaten up by a German policeman.)

A policeman sat in the back of the lorry with Gray and his morose companion while a civilian did the driving. They travelled along the eastern bank of what Gray guessed was the Rhine, crossed the famous bridge at Remagen and came to a halt outside the town's police station. (Later, Gray guessed that he had been picked up in Konigswinter, just SE of Bonn, from where he was driven to Remagen.)

Immediately inside the police station, Gray was accosted by an ageing policeman, excitedly waving a newspaper. The paper told of shattering Allied losses on the Nuremberg raid. Gray's reaction was to dismiss the report as 'Goebbels' propaganda', although the RAF did in fact suffer very heavily indeed on the night of 30 March.

...a hole filled with blood

But the ancient *politzei* kept on jabbering and pointing to Gray's eyes. Gray walked over to a mirror in the corner. No wonder his original captors were scared stiff! The make-up man for a horror movie could never have done a better job. In the middle of each huge black eye was a hole filled with blood. The force of Gray's landing must have burst all the blood vessels in the eye-balls. The explanation is simple, but the effect was frighteningly macabre—yet he felt no discomfort.

All the staff at the police station stared fearfully at Gray as he and W.O. Hall were taken to the cell block and locked up. Hall was still as silent as ever and was in obvious distress. Gray rolled up his Irvine jacket to serve as a pillow and laid Hall onto it. Whimpers and low moans were coming from one of the neighboring cells. The noise was beginning to get on Gray's nerves when the cell door opened and four scruffy and dispirited RAF officers and NCOs entered. They were accompanied by a pale little fellow with only one leg and dressed in a combination of civilian clothing and American uniform.

Gray managed to persuade the guard to bring them all some food, but despite this and his own battered countenance, the newcomers looked at him with undisguised suspicion and whispered among themselves. The afternoon passed in gloomy silence, broken only by the whimpering from the next cell.

A party of *Luftwaffe* personnel arrived at about 1700 and took Gray and his companions to a lorry parked outside. They were driven to the town's railway station. Fortunately, the officer in charge knew a little English and Gray pointed out Hall's condition to him. He was not unsympathetic and helped Hall up beside the driver—borrowing Gray's Irvine jacket to keep the patient warm.

As the prisoners climbed down at the railway station, the officer in charge signalled to Hall to stay where he was. That was the last Gray ever saw of his Irvine jacket or of Hall.

The prisoners—minus Hall—were escorted to one of the station platforms. As they stood there an air-raid siren wailed its warning. Soon, a flight of Me 109s took off from a nearby airfield and passed over the station. Gray had been flying for three years, yet these were the first enemy planes he had ever seen.

A train drew in and the prisoners were hustled aboard. There followed a slow but fairly comfortable journey to Frankfurt-on-Main. His guards were entertained with

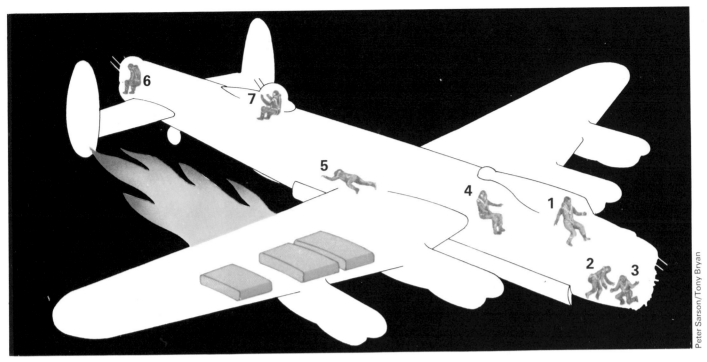

Peter Sarson/Tony Bryan

Diagrammatic arrangement of oxygen equipment

1 Gas cylinder
2 Main cock
3 High pressure pipeline (copper)
4 Regulator with a. Supply gauge
   b. Altitude gauge
5 Low pressure pipeline (light alloy)
6 Manifold
7 Cut off valve
8 Bayonet joint socket stowage clip
9 Flow indicator
10 Economiser
11 Flexible pipe (reinforced fabric)
12 Bayonet joint plug and socket
13 Oxygen mask

The Last Moments of T-Tare

With her starboard wing blazing, the Lancaster was out of control and in a near-vertical dive. After giving the 'Bale out!' order, and receiving acknowledgements, the pilot (1), W.O. Donald Gray, left his seat to open the bomb-doors. Searing heat and light met him. How he left the stricken bomber remains a mystery. But he reached the ground by the hazardous method of hanging by his ankles from his parachute harness. Only two other crew members survived, the navigator (2), Flt. Sgt. Alan Campbell, and the bomb-aimer (3), Flt. Sgt. George Wallis.

The positions of the rest of the crew, as they were last known, were the radio-op (4), Sgt. Bert Wright, at his set; the flight engineer (5), Sgt. Joseph Grant, in the fuselage unconscious; the rear-gunner (6), Sgt. Douglas Maugham, unconscious, and the mid-upper gunner (7), Sgt. Frank Patey, in his turret. None of them survived.

◁ The life support, necessary at altitude. The rear-gunner and flight engineer both had problems with oxygen. Fixtures under pressure can be subject to failure.

▷ The standard air-crew parachute harness.

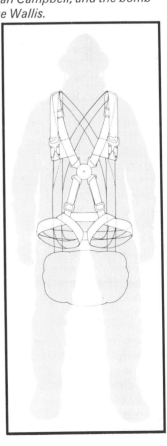

Davis & Harrison VP Ltd

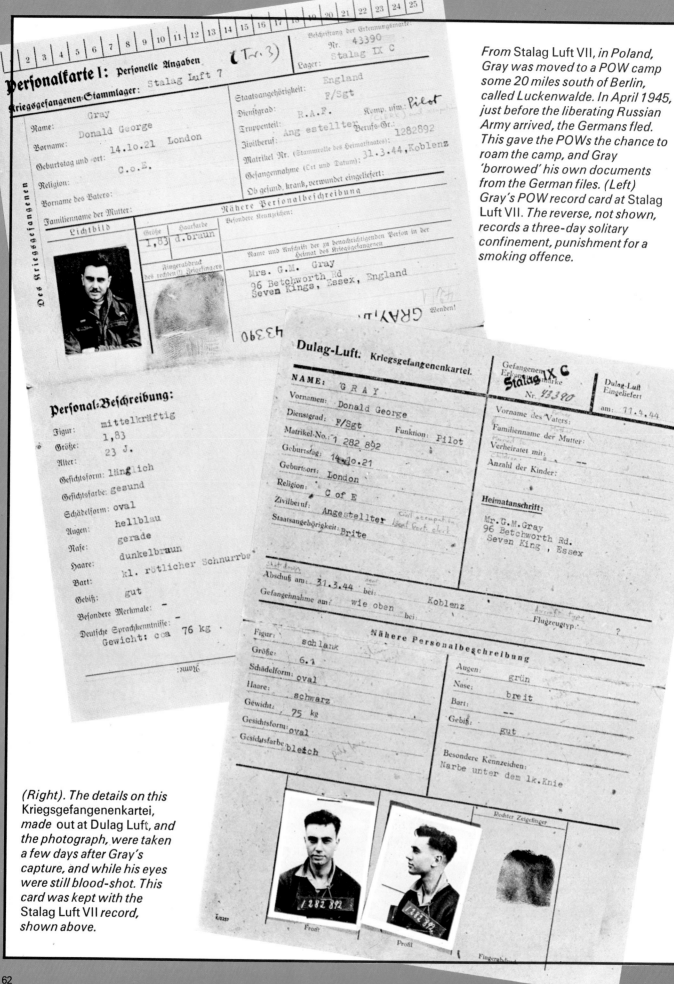

From Stalag Luft VII, *in Poland,
Gray was moved to a POW camp
some 20 miles south of Berlin,
called Luckenwalde. In April 1945,
just before the liberating Russian
Army arrived, the Germans fled.
This gave the POWs the chance to
roam the camp, and Gray
'borrowed' his own documents
from the German files. (Left)
Gray's POW record card at Stalag
Luft VII. The reverse, not shown,
records a three-day solitary
confinement, punishment for a
smoking offence.*

(Right). The details on this
Kriegsgefangenenkartei, *made
out at Dulag Luft, and
the photograph, were taken
a few days after Gray's
capture, and while his eyes
were still blood-shot. This
card was kept with the
Stalag Luft VII record,
shown above.*

songs sung by a woman in military uniform. Gray reflected that only nine days previously he had been on the raid which had pulverized this city. It would not have been wise to let his captors in on the secret.

By now, it was pretty late in the evening and the prisoners were taken to a large public air-raid shelter to spend the night.

Next morning, Gray was rudely awakened by a nudge in the ribs from a jackboot, and a bad-tempered grunt. It was a splendid Sunday morning as the prisoners were herded aboard an articulated tram for the journey to the *Auswertestelle West* ('Evaluation center for the West') camp at Oberursel for interrogation.

Oberursel was a hastily erected complex of huts, bounded by a barbed wire fence. On arrival, all the prisoners were searched and taken away one by one.

Gray found himself in a small room, furnished with a radiator, a crudely fashioned timber bed, a straw mattress and an old blanket. These quarters were lit by a frosted glass window. Suddenly, the door burst open. An insignificant gentleman, in glasses and uniform, stalked in. He gave Gray a pencil and a form, turned on his heels and stalked out again—saying in impeccable English as he went that he would collect the completed form later.

Across the top of the form was the legend 'International Red Cross'. Gray and his comrades had been warned by RAF Intelligence that it was no such thing. All the questions seemed to concern only military matters. Accordingly, Gray filled in his name, rank and number and crossed through the remaining sections.

This behavior did not, of course, endear him to his captors—although they were probably used to non-co-operation from newly arrived prisoners. Gray spent four days in solitary confinement. He was given to understand that if he decided to toe the line, he would have to arrange an interview with his interrogators. They were in no hurry.

Lack of food, washing facilities and medical attention took their toll. All this, coupled with boredom, uncertainty and the deliberately contrived 'erratic' radiator in his cell, took Gray's morale down to its lowest ebb.

At the end of this ordeal, a second interview took place. Gray's interrogators handed him a book which appeared to contain a full list of RAF squadrons and their personnel. He noticed a reference to his squadron, No. 50, and saw some aircrew names but showed no recognition. He then lingered over a page containing details of a Spitfire squadron. They then threatened to have Gray shot as a spy because he could not prove his identity. After this performance he was sent back to his cell.

There he remained for a further two days, when his chief interrogator and a fat middle-aged officer entered his cell. This man displayed concern over the condition of Gray's eyes and left. That afternoon, the bandage on his leg was changed for the first time since his capture. He was then driven to a mansion about a mile distant. This had been turned into a hospital for injured Allied aircrew. The medical orderlies here were Allied POWs.

Here, and in two other hospitals, he was nursed to recovery. After 10 weeks of treatment Gray was interned at *Stalag Luft VII*. It was not until a year later that he learned, in a letter from his mother, dated October 1944, that his navigator and bomb aimer had survived.

Gray also spent the rest of the war as a POW. Unlucky? Perhaps, but then it was a miracle that he was alive.

Paul Hutchinson

THE TWO OTHER SURVIVORS

When W.O. Gray gave the 'Bail out!' order, the navigator, Flt. Sgt. Alan Campbell, clipped on his parachute and left his compartment to make his way forward to the bomb-aimer's position in the nose of the Lancaster. Through the pilot's window he could see long tongues of blue and yellow flame streaming back from the starboard wing and reaching almost to the tail. The bomb-aimer, Flt. Sgt. George Wallis, was trying to open the escape hatch, but it wouldn't move. As he threw up his hands in a gesture of failure there was a 'Whomp!' and Campbell was propelled forward, down the steps into the plane's nose.

As he was thrown forward he hit something hard. There was pressure, flame, disorientation, then—nothing.

He opened his eyes. The stars were above: all was quiet, no sound, no sense of motion. Not certain whether he was clear of the aircraft, he pulled the ripcord anyway. 'Wonderful! The chute opened with a jerk and I was floating. I looked up and in the moonlight I could see that glorious great canopy billowing above me!' Below Campbell was another parachute. Good, someone else was out too.

The Flt. Sgt. landed in a quiet German countryside. The time by his watch was 0030. Above, he could hear the familiar whine of Merlin-engined Lancasters on their way to Nuremberg.

Campbell was in fair shape. A cut head, facial scratches, swollen right arm, sore knee and a painful kidney were a small price for getting out of a blazing Lancaster, and coming to earth by parachute.

Traditionally, a flier buries his parachute to avoid the great expanse of white nylon being spotted as tell-tale evidence of the crewman's presence. But it was tangled in bushes and Campbell gave up the task of getting it out of sight. He cut pieces off as souvenirs, and headed west towards the Rhine.

Then a figure loomed up. Guessing it was an armed German, Campbell raised his hands, explaining he was an RAF navigator from a shot-down Lancaster. But the figure placed a hand on the Flt. Sgt.'s shoulder and said: 'Don't panic, Al. It's me, George!' It was the Lancaster's bomb-aimer, Flt. Sgt. George Wallis, who had escaped through the shattered perspex of the aircraft's nose after the explosion.

The two crewmen headed for the Rhine, but it was not long before they were spotted and escorted to a police station in Neuweid, on the east bank of the Rhine north of Koblenz.

From there they were sent to the Interrogation Center at Oberursel and final to *Stalagluft VI*, at Heydekrug, on the Baltic, where they arrived on Easter Sunday, 1944, to await the end of the war and liberation.